Alcohol and Drug Counselor Exam
Practice Questions

Mometrix
TEST PREPARATION

Dear Future Exam Success Story

First of all, **THANK YOU** for purchasing Mometrix study materials!

Second, congratulations! You are one of the few determined test-takers who are committed to doing whatever it takes to excel on your exam. **You have come to the right place.** We developed these practice tests with one goal in mind: to deliver you the best possible approximation of the questions you will see on test day.

Standardized testing is one of the biggest obstacles on your road to success, which only increases the importance of doing well in the high-pressure, high-stakes environment of test day. Your results on this test could have a significant impact on your future, and these practice tests will give you the repetitions you need to build your familiarity and confidence with the test content and format to help you achieve your full potential on test day.

Your success is our success

We would love to hear from you! If you would like to share the story of your exam success or if you have any questions or comments in regard to our products, please contact us at **800-673-8175** or **support@mometrix.com**.

Thanks again for your business and we wish you continued success!

Sincerely,
The Mometrix Test Preparation Team

TABLE OF CONTENTS

Practice Test #1

1. A wife refers her husband for substance abuse counseling. His drug of choice is cocaine, which he has been using episodically with friends at a poker game—biweekly to weekly—for some years. She is disturbed at the illicit nature of the drug and the long-standing use. He states that though he recreationally uses, he doesn't crave cocaine, doesn't seek it out but rather uses with friends at the game who bring it. He feels that other than his wife being upset, he has no other social or occupational issues. Given the information provided, how is his use of cocaine BEST described?

    a. Substance abuse
    b. Cocaine intoxication
    c. Cocaine use disorder
    d. None of the above

2. What does the experienced effect of a drug depend upon?

    a. The amount taken and past drug experiences
    b. The modality of administration
    c. Poly drug use, setting, and circumstance
    d. All of the above

3. How is drug tolerance BEST described?

    a. The inability to get intoxicated
    b. The need for more of a drug to get intoxicated
    c. Increased sensitivity to a drug over time
    d. Decreased sensitivity to a drug over time

4. Which of the following is NOT a "drug cue"?

    a. A prior drug-use setting
    b. Drug use paraphernalia
    c. Seeing others use drugs
    d. Drug avoidance strategies

5. What happens as tolerance for barbiturates develops?

    a. The margin between intoxication and lethality increases.
    b. The margin between intoxication and lethality decreases.
    c. The margin between intoxication and lethality stays the same.
    d. Tolerance does not develop for barbiturates.

6. What is the MOST common symptom of Wernicke's encephalopathy?

    a. New memory formation
    b. Loss of older memories
    c. Psychosis
    d. Confusion

7. Which of the following conditions does alcohol NOT induce?

    a. Steatosis
    b. Nephrosis
    c. Hepatitis
    d. Cirrhosis

8. What does formication refer to?

    a. The creation of freebase cocaine
    b. Sex between two unmarried individuals
    c. A sensation of bugs crawling under the skin
    d. Extrapyramidal symptoms of agitation

9. What is/are the organ(s) most damaged by cocaine abuse?

    a. The brain
    b. The lungs
    c. The kidneys
    d. The heart

10. Which of the following is NOT a basic chemical class of amphetamines?

    a. Amphetamine sulphate
    b. Benzedrine
    c. Dextroamphetamine
    d. Methamphetamine

11. In terms of difficulty quitting (dependence), which of the following four drugs ranks the highest?

    a. Alcohol
    b. Cocaine
    c. Heroin
    d. Nicotine

12. Which of the statements below is MOST correct?

    a. THC content in all marijuana is about the same.
    b. THC content in hashish is lower than in a joint.
    c. THC content in marijuana is predictable.
    d. THC content in marijuana varies widely.

13. Regarding substance abuse, what does Convergence Theory propose?

    a. Rates of substance abuse among women are converging with those of men.
    b. All individuals eventually narrow drug use to a drug of choice preference.
    c. Age is a key factor in eventual substance abuse abstinence.
    d. As individuals age, gender disparities in rates of abuse tend to converge.

14. Among psychiatric disorders in the elderly, where does alcohol abuse rank?

    a. twenty-fifth
    b. fifteenth
    c. fifth
    d. third

2

15. Which of the following subcategories of alcohol use disorder onset is NOT found in the elderly?

    a. Late-onset alcoholism
    b. Delayed-onset alcoholism
    c. Late-onset exacerbation drinking
    d. Early-onset alcoholism

16. At an initial meeting with a new client, what is the FIRST requirement?

    a. Establish rapport.
    b. Evaluate readiness for change.
    c. Review rules and expectations.
    d. Discuss confidentiality regulations.

17. What does motivational interviewing primarily involve?

    a. Focused confrontation
    b. Behavioral accountability
    c. Reality testing
    d. Supportive persuasion

18. What percentage of individuals with a dual diagnosis (co-occurring disorders [COD]—i.e., substance abuse disorder and an existing mental illness) received treatment for only their mental illness?

    a. 32.9 percent
    b. 27.6 percent
    c. 12.4 percent
    d. 8.8 percent

19. What factors can affect screening instrument validity?

    a. The screening setting and privacy
    b. The levels of rapport and trust
    c. How instructions are given and clarified
    d. All of the above

20. Which of the following functions is NOT what a Certified Alcohol and Drug Abuse Counselor can usually perform?

    a. Client screening
    b. Substance abuse assessment
    c. Diagnose mental disorders
    d. Formulate a treatment plan

21. What does the acronym GATE stand for?

    a. Gather information; Access supervision; Take responsible action; Extend the action
    b. Gather resources; Access procedures; Take clinical notes; Extend the intervention
    c. Gather documentation; Access contacts; Take counsel; Extend positive outcomes
    d. Gather the team; Access records; Take consultation; Extend documentation

22. To which of the following do assessment processes and instruments NOT need be sensitive?

a. Political orientation
b. Age and gender
c. Race and ethnicity
d. Disabilities

23. What are serious mental health symptoms that resolve with abstinence in thirty days or less MOST likely due to?

a. A resolution of transient situational stressors at home, school, or work
b. A serious underlying mental disorder that temporarily improved
c. Substance abuse-induced disorders that require continued abstinence
d. Malingering to manipulate circumstances for underlying goals

24. Which one of the following alcohol abuse screening tests is designed specifically for use with adolescents?

a. CAGE
b. CRAFFT
c. MAST
d. AUDIT

25. Which of the following is the MOST important introductory statement or question to ask in a suicidality evaluation?

a. Have you ever tried to take your own life?
b. Do you have thoughts about killing yourself?
c. I need to ask you a few questions about suicide.
d. Have you ever attempted suicide?

26. What is the purpose of screening?

a. To prepare the client for program admission
b. To determine client readiness for change
c. To establish client diagnoses and treatment needs
d. To determine the need for placement or referral

27. What is the primary purpose of substance abuse assessment?

a. To determine the current level of health deterioration
b. To identify a substance abuser's drug of choice
c. To provide co-occurring disorder(s) diagnosis
d. To determine the severity of the substance problem

28. Who should create a treatment plan?

a. A multidisciplinary team of professionals
b. Collaborative team with the client
c. The primary treatment provider
d. A professional boilerplate to ensure completeness

4

29. How must assessment information be handled to be the MOST effective?
   a. Carefully documented
   b. Converted into goals and objectives
   c. Available to all treatment providers
   d. Summarized with the client for feedback

30. Which of these key elements does NOT bolster a client's desire to complete the program?
   a. Knowledge of the benefits of treatment
   b. Understanding of the treatment process
   c. Fully assuming the patient role
   d. Frequent interdisciplinary consultations

31. How many levels of treatment placement are recognized by the American Society of Addiction Medicine (ASAM)?
   a. Two levels of treatment placement
   b. Four levels of treatment placement
   c. Six levels of treatment placement
   d. Eight levels of treatment placement

32. How many Assessment Dimensions are recognized by the American Society of Addiction Medicine (ASAM)?
   a. Two assessment dimensions
   b. Four assessment dimensions
   c. Six assessment dimensions
   d. Eight assessment dimensions

33. The term "drug use trajectory" refers to:
   a. Individual drug use patterns over the lifespan
   b. The rate at which a given drug enters the body
   c. Drug metabolism over time
   d. Behavioral patterns of intoxication

34. Circumstances, Motivation, Readiness, and Suitability (CMRS) Scales are used for what purpose?
   a. Assessing client readiness for treatment
   b. Assessing various financial and family support domains
   c. Assessing client suitability for research participation
   d. Assessing clients for treatment level of care

35. When is a client fully prepared to enter treatment?
   a. Treatment is court ordered.
   b. Family pressures a client to enter treatment.
   c. Job-based drug testing creates a clear need.
   d. A client accepts the need for treatment.

36. Guiding principles in treatment planning are identified by which acronym?
    a. MTSRA
    b. MATRS
    c. MSRTA
    d. MRAST

37. In cases involving the criminal justice system, what is the minimum recommendation for frequency of updating treatment plans?
    a. Following sentencing
    b. Upon release to a community setting
    c. At all transition points
    d. Both A and B

38. How many problem domains are addressed in the Addiction Severity Index (ASI)?
    a. Six
    b. Eight
    c. Ten
    d. Twelve

39. The Addiction Severity Index has been formally adopted by which organization?
    a. The Substance Abuse and Mental Health Services Administration (SAMHSA)
    b. The Center on Drug and Alcohol Research (CDAR)
    c. The National Institute on Drug Abuse (NIDA)
    d. The Institute for Governmental Service and Research (IGSR)

40. What does it mean if an assessment instrument is valid?
    a. The instrument is licensed for use by professionals.
    b. The instrument consistently provides accurate information.
    c. The instrument has been approved by the government for use.
    d. The instrument assesses what it purports to assess.

41. All of the following are true of depression and substance abuse EXCEPT that
    a. drugs of abuse can successfully treat depression.
    b. depression can lead to self-medication with drugs of abuse.
    c. drugs of abuse can induce symptoms of depression.
    d. drugs of abuse can worsen symptoms of depression.

42. How does motivation for participating in treatment differ from motivation to change behaviors?
    a. There is no difference between treatment and behavior change motivation.
    b. Motivation for behavioral change precedes motivation for treatment.
    c. Motivation for change is internal; treatment may be pushed on a client.
    d. Motivation for treatment precedes motivation for behavioral change.

43. What of the following is NOT a key component in a treatment plan?
    a. Problem statements from the intake assessment
    b. Goal statements derived from problem statements
    c. Objectives, which are what the client will do to meet treatment goals
    d. The theoretical approach to be operationalized via treatment

44. What does the SOAP progress note acronym stand for?

   a. Subjective, Overview, Actions, and Plan
   b. Subjective, Objective, Assessment, and Plan
   c. Subjective, Observation, Assessment, and Plan
   d. Subjective, Overview, Attention, and Plan

45. What does the DAP progress note acronym stand for?

   a. Description, Assessment, and Progress
   b. Details, Assessment, and Progress
   c. Documentation, Actions, and Pending
   d. Data, Assessment, and Plan

46. The mnemonic DIG-FAST evaluates which psychological state?

   a. Depression
   b. Anxiety
   c. Paranoia
   d. Mania

47. How does the Center for Substance Abuse Treatment (CSAT) recommend that substance abuse be considered and treated?

   a. A psychological disorder
   b. An acute disease
   c. A chronic treatable condition
   d. A degenerative treatable disorder

48. How does the Center for Substance Abuse Treatment (CSAT) indicate that treatment or interventions provided following discharge from a formal inpatient or outpatient program be referred to?

   a. After care
   b. Continuing care
   c. Follow-up care
   d. Post-discharge care

49. What is the BEST distinction between substance abuse treatment programs and mutual-help groups, such as a twelve-step support groups?

   a. Programs offer help, and groups offer support.
   b. Programs are expensive, and groups are free.
   c. Programs are run by professionals, and groups are run by laypersons.
   d. Programs offer treatment, and groups offer support.

50. According to the American Society of Addiction Medicine (ASAM), what is the minimum of treatment time the intensive outpatient treatment (IOT) must provide?

   a. Three hours of treatment per week
   b. Six hours of treatment per week
   c. Nine hours of treatment per week
   d. Twelve hours of treatment per week

7

51. **Which of the following is NOT a core feature or service that the Center for Substance Abuse Treatment (CSAT) consensus panel agreed upon?**

    a. Biopsychosocial assessment
    b. Individualized treatment planning
    c. Case management
    d. Recreational therapy

52. **Which form of substance abuse is naltrexone used to treat?**

    a. Alcohol dependence
    b. Opioid dependence
    c. Both A and B
    d. Neither A nor B

53. **Which of the following is NOT a core treatment and recovery skill?**

    a. Stress management
    b. Substance refusal training
    c. Exercise and health training
    d. Relaxation training

54. **Which of the following is NOT a primary learning style?**

    a. Gustatory
    b. Kinesthetic
    c. Auditory
    d. Visual

55. **What is the influence of family on treatment outcomes?**

    a. Treatment outcomes are improved with family support.
    b. Treatment outcomes are worse with family involvement.
    c. Both A and B
    d. Neither A nor B

56. **How many main levels exist in the substance abuse continuum of care, according to the American Society of Addiction Medicine (ASAM)?**

    a. Three levels of care
    b. Four levels of care
    c. Five levels of care
    d. Six levels of care

57. **How many sequential stages must outpatient clients work through, regardless of the level of care at which they enter treatment?**

    a. Two stages
    b. Four stages
    c. Six stages
    d. Eight stages

58. What is the usual recommended minimum duration of days for the intensive outpatient treatment (IOT) phase?

    a. Thirty days
    b. Sixty days
    c. Ninety days   3 months
    d. One hundred twenty days

59. How is the MOST effective relapse-prevention training provided?

    a. Group therapy is more effective.
    b. Individual therapy is more effective.
    c. Structured classes are more effective.
    d. A and B are roughly equal in effectiveness.

60. Which of the following is NOT a type of intensive outpatient treatment (IOT) group?

    a. Psychoeducational groups
    b. Skills development groups
    c. Interpersonal process groups
    d. Transitional care groups

61. What is the MOST common duration of counseling in an intensive outpatient treatment (IOT) program?

    a. Twenty to thirty minutes, one time each week
    b. Thirty to fifty minutes, one time each week
    c. Forty to sixty minutes, one time each week
    d. Thirty to fifty minutes, two times each week

62. How are pharmacotherapy and medication management in substance abuse treatment described?

    a. Of little importance outside a hospitalization program
    b. Of some but limited value but without a central role
    c. Of moderate value in treatment but not crucial
    d. Of considerable, albeit limited, value in treatment

63. Topics addressed in psychoeducational groups are typically

    a. sequenced by concept for maximal effectiveness.
    b. presented as requested or needed by group participants.
    c. selected randomly by the group educator or presenter.
    d. determined by the group's prevailing drug of choice.

64. What was the original CIWA-Ar scale designed for?

    a. Evaluation of opioid withdrawal risk
    b. Evaluation of amphetamine withdrawal risk
    c. Evaluation of alcohol withdrawal risk
    d. Evaluation of benzodiazepine withdrawal risk

65. Which of the following substances lack effective treatment medications?

a. Cocaine
b. Marijuana
c. Both of the above
d. Neither of the above

66. Adjunctive therapies refer to all EXCEPT which of the following?

a. Vocational training
b. Stress management
c. Meditation
d. Acupuncture

67. Dealing with smoking cessation during a substance abuse treatment program is

a. something too overwhelming for the majority of individuals.
b. something that should not be brought up by anyone but the client.
c. something to be seriously considered if the client desires it.
d. something that should be required during any treatment program.

68. Disulfiram (Antabuse) is contraindicated for clients whose alcohol abuse is combined with which of the following circumstances?

a. Cocaine use
b. Methadone use
c. Both cocaine and methadone use
d. None of the above

69. What is the sandwich technique?

a. A method to increase health food intake
b. An intake interviewing technique
c. Client pairing for optimal treatment support
d. Staff pairing for optimal treatment support

70. Which of the following was NOT identified as being among the three MOST effective screening tools for substance use disorders?

a. The CSAT Simple Screening Instrument
b. The Alcohol Dependence Scale (ADS) and the Addiction Severity Index (ASI)-Drug Use Subscale combined
c. The Substance Abuse Screening Instrument
d. The Texas Christian University Drug Screen

71. What is the SDSS designed to measure?

a. Substance-induced depression over time
b. Variations in polysubstance use over time
c. Drug use disorder severity over time
d. Severity and duration of intoxication symptoms

72. **What is the primary purpose of the Texas Christian University Drug Screen (TCUDS)?**

    a. To identify those with versus those without issues of drug dependency
    b. To establish a roster of the kinds and severity of drugs used in the past
    c. To evaluate dangerousness and risk taking in drug use patterns
    d. To correlate drug use patterns with emerging health concerns

73. **What is physiological dependence on a drug determined by?**

    a. The addictive properties of the drug
    b. Tolerance or symptoms of withdrawal
    c. A psychological need to again use the drug
    d. Frequency and amount of the drug taken

74. **According the DSM-5 criteria, a client that has previously met the criteria for stimulant use disorder but now has not met the criteria for stimulant use in 10 months (except for craving) would be termed to be in _____ remission.**

    a. Full
    b. Partial
    c. Early
    d. Sustained

75. **What is a client's family of choice used to describe?**

    a. Step-parents and step- and half-siblings
    b. Common-law relationships only
    c. Planned pregnancies as opposed to those unplanned
    d. Relationships created by marriage, friendship, and other associations

76. **What does a dual relationship refer to?**

    a. Dyads assigned in addiction-recovery groups for added support
    b. The sponsor–sponsee relationship in twelve-step groups such as A.A.
    c. The mentor relationship with those newly entering addiction treatments
    d. A working relationship with a client outside the professional domain

77. **What is an appropriate response to a substantial gift from a client?**

    a. "You shouldn't have!"
    b. "Thank you so much!"
    c. "I can't accept that, but thank you!"
    d. "A gift like that is not appropriate."

78. **Two clients in a treatment group begin dating. What would a proper response be?**

    a. Address program policy preventing dating among group members.
    b. Initiate a group activity to acknowledge their new relationship.
    c. Terminate treatment for both of the members.
    d. Terminate treatment for one of the members.

79. At a local dance club, a counselor spots a client drinking at the bar. What is the BEST response to this?

    a. Confront the client immediately, encouraging him or her to leave the club.
    b. Quietly find a moment to talk with the client privately at the club.
    c. Avoid contact with the client, and leave the club immediately.
    d. Avoid contact with the client, but remain at the club.

80. As a substance abuse counselor, you work in a treatment program and also personally attend a twelve-step program in the community. A treatment program client asks you to become his or her twelve-step sponsor. What is the proper, thoughtful response?

    a. Accept, knowing that it may benefit the therapeutic alliance.
    b. Accept, knowing how much this client needs help.
    c. Decline, concerned that the client could be difficult to support.
    d. Decline, recognizing the potential conflicts in multiple roles.

81. In providing counseling treatment, what are counselors encouraged to do?

    a. Select a single counseling approach, and refine it fully.
    b. Use multiple counseling approaches to meet clients' needs.
    c. Avoid relying on any formal counseling technique.
    d. Recognize that all counseling techniques are equally effective.

82. What does the Twelve-Step Facilitation Approach refer to?

    a. Program counselors also serving as twelve-step group facilitators
    b. Twelve-step program facilitators working within a treatment program
    c. Teaching twelve-step principles during treatment program work
    d. Encouraging clients to enter a community twelve-step program

83. Which of the following is NOT a strength of twelve-step programs?

    a. Twelve-step meetings are free, widely available, and offer ongoing support.
    b. The twelve-step approach easily accommodates client diversity.
    c. Twelve-step programs offer easy monitoring of assigned step tasks.
    d. The twelve-step approach offers recovery in cognitive, health, and spiritual areas.

84. Staff familiarity with twelve-step program facilitation is important because of all of the following EXCEPT that

    a. clients feel more pressure to attend twelve-step programs by these staff.
    b. clients are more easily motivated into twelve-step programs by these staff.
    c. clients' concerns are more meaningfully resolved by these staff.
    d. clients generally remain abstinent longer with twelve-step involvement.

85. When outcomes from cognitive-behavioral coping skills therapy and motivational enhancement therapy are compared with outcomes from twelve-step facilitation, how do clients fare BEST?

    a. cognitive-behavioral coping skills therapy
    b. motivational enhancement therapy
    c. Twelve-step facilitation
    d. All the above

86. Traditionally, what has the term *therapeutic community (TC)* referred to?

    a. An informal group organized for mutual support
    b. A court-ordered treatment environment
    c. A formal mutual-help or twelve-step support group
    d. A drug-free residential treatment environment

87. Why do therapeutic communities (TCs) often focus on habilitation instead of rehabilitation?

    a. Many clients cannot successfully be rehabilitated.
    b. Rehabilitation is not as effective as habilitation.
    c. Habilitation helps clients learn new skills they never had.
    d. Rehabilitation focuses only narrowly on detoxification.

88. In what setting is the therapeutic community (TC) treatment model MOST effective?

    a. A formal full-time residential setting
    b. An intensive day treatment setting
    c. Neither A nor B, but in a support group setting
    d. A and B equally

89. What is the MOST important reason that ordered and routine activities are built into the therapeutic community (TC) treatment process?

    a. To relieve boredom that may serve as a trigger for substance abuse
    b. To counter the typically disordered lives of substance-abusing clients
    c. To reduce the stress through focused programmed activities
    d. To distract from the negative thinking that may lead to substance abuse

90. What is the Matrix Model designed to treat?

    a. Stimulant abuse
    b. Alcohol abuse
    c. Barbiturate abuse
    d. Inhalant abuse

91. Which of the following is not a drawback to community reinforcement (CR) and contingency management (CM) approaches?

    a. CR and CM are most effective if used together.
    b. CR and CM are not enduringly effective.
    c. CR is labor intensive, and CM can be costly.
    d. CR requires others' support, and CM requires ongoing rewards.

92. With regard to co-occurring disorders, what does the term integrated treatment refer to?

    a. Meeting both medical and substance abuse treatment needs
    b. Using an eclectic treatment paradigm in the treatment process
    c. Incorporating sociocultural issues in the treatment process
    d. Treating both psychiatric and substance abuse issues concurrently

93. What would be the MOST typical co-occurring disorder client?

    a. An alcohol-abusing man
    b. A drug-abusing man
    c. An alcohol-abusing woman
    d. A drug-abusing woman

94. How many categories does SAMHSA's Service Coordination Framework for Co-Occurring Disorders have?

    a. Two categories
    b. Four categories
    c. Six categories
    d. Eight categories

95. When behaviorally assessing for a co-occurring disorder, what is the MOST important variable to consider?

    a. Alcohol or drug toxicity or withdrawal symptoms
    b. The client's denial of any psychiatric problems
    c. The client's family history of psychiatric disorders
    d. The client's immediate behavior

96. How are substance abuse treatment programs for adolescents described?

    a. Very different from treatment programs for adults
    b. Somewhat different from treatment programs for adults
    c. Minimally different from treatment programs for adults
    d. Not at all different from treatment programs for adults

97. What is the MOST effective treatment approach for adolescents, in terms of less drug use at treatment completion?

    a. Parent education
    b. Peer group therapy
    c. Family therapy
    d. Multifamily interventions

98. How is the concept of culture BEST described?

    a. A shared set of beliefs, norms, and values among a racial group
    b. A shared set of beliefs, norms, and values among an ethnic group
    c. A shared set of beliefs, norms, and values among any given group
    d. A shared set of beliefs, norms, and values among a given nationality

99. Who is primarily responsible for ensuring that treatment is effective for culturally diverse clients?

    a. The client
    b. The provider
    c. The institution
    d. The family

100. What does the term *culture-bound syndrome* refer to?

 a. An illness (mental or physical) unique to a cultural group
 b. An illness presenting or interpreted distinctively, due to cultural influence
 c. Both A and B
 d. Neither A nor B

101. Beyond the culture of the client, what is another key cultural issue?

 a. Client's number of generations in the United States
 b. Clients living in cultural enclaves
 c. Culture of the counselor
 d. Client's primary language

102. What are the two key mental health treatment paradigms of Western medicine?

 a. Objectivity and the scientific method
 b. Theoretical and applied practice
 c. Pharmacological therapy and psychotherapy
 d. Biological and environmental perspectives

103. Racism may jeopardize the mental health of minorities in all of the following ways EXCEPT that

 a. negative racial images and stereotypes adversely affect social and psychological function.
 b. racism and discrimination result in diminished socioeconomic status, where poverty, crime, and violence affect mental health.
 c. racism and discrimination lead to physiological changes and psychological distress that affect mental health.
 d. discrimination and racism limit recreational and leisure opportunities to improve mental health.

104. What is the trend for cultural diversity in the United States?

 a. Decreasing slowly but steadily
 b. Remaining approximately unchanged
 c. Increasing slowly but steadily
 d. Increasing rapidly and steadily

105. What is the difference between AIDS and HIV?

 a. HIV can be fatal; AIDS is a nonfatal chronic condition.
 b. HIV is a common viral illness, while AIDS is a lethal infection.
 c. HIV is the virus that causes the AIDS syndrome.
 d. HIV is sexually transmitted, while AIDS is acquired in other ways.

106. As compared with current older adults, what is the upcoming baby boomer generation (born between 1946 and 1964) expected to have?

 a. Much lower treatment needs
 b. Somewhat lower treatment needs
 c. Somewhat higher treatment needs
 d. Much higher treatment needs

107. When older adults enter treatment, how do their rates of attendance and incidence of relapse, compare to their younger cohorts?

a. Much higher attendance and much lower relapse rates
b. Somewhat higher attendance and modestly lower relapse rates
c. No real difference in attendance or relapse rates
d. Much lower attendance and much higher relapse rates

108. Confidentiality requirements exist to protect client's and their personal lives and information. Without a client signed information release, what is information that can be disclosed?

a. A client's enrollment in a treatment program only
b. A report of child abuse suspected to be caused by the client
c. A client's name, age, gender, and race or ethnicity
d. A report of progress to an employer paying for treatment

109. The CAGE questionnaire is a four-question screening tool. What is this screening instrument designed to screen for?

a. Cocaine abuse
b. Marijuana abuse
c. Alcohol abuse
d. Heroin abuse

110. The MAST screening test is a twenty-five-question instrument that is used to explore the degree and severity of a client's problem with which type of abuse?

a. Cocaine abuse
b. Mescaline abuse
c. Methamphetamine abuse
d. Alcohol abuse

111. The relapse and remitting model addresses cycles of relapse and recovery common to addiction. What else can it be usefully applied to?

a. Medication management
b. Unemployment
c. Issues of anger and violence
d. All of the above

112. The term *authentically connected referral network* is used in conjunction with case management. How is it BEST defined?

a. A resource directory of available community services to call as needed
b. A set of defined relationships able to adapt and flexibly meet client needs
c. A rolodex with key names and contacts for needed services
d. An informal consortium of providers sharing information among each other

113. In providing case management services, beyond providing seamless care and being client focused, what is the primary aim?

a. Provide referrals to needed services in as timely a way as possible
b. Determine how to integrate needed referrals in a coordinated fashion
c. Produce the least-restrictive level of care possible in meeting the client's needs
d. Promote client self-determination in identifying and selecting needed services

114. Sensitive interviewing and engagement techniques are important to optimize client responsiveness and investment. What does the ask-tell-ask technique refer to?

a. Asking permission of the client to talk with them, telling them of any concerns you have, and then asking for their thoughts on what you shared

b. Asking clients what they understand, telling them where they are wrong, and asking again if they understand

c. Asking clients for their opinions, telling them where their opinions are valid and workable, and then asking them if they concur

d. Asking clients to listen, telling them what they need to know, and asking if they will acquiesce to what is being asked of them

115. After referrals are made, it is important to track the associated outcomes for measures of referral success. What are the three MOST important evaluative aspects?

a. How, where, and when

b. Why, what, and where

c. Where, when, and who

d. Who, what, and how

116. Given a client's history, referrals for co-occurring disorders as well as medical, educational, and psychological needs should be ongoing as discovered. When should planning for aftercare be engaged?

a. During the last few sessions, addressing specific, continuing needs

b. When a client is roughly halfway through a program

c. After measurable progress has been demonstrated

d. At the point of the initial counselor–client contact

117. Education regarding substance abuse includes topics such as triggers, patterns of abuse, and relapse prevention. What should treatment MOSTLY be focused on?

a. Substance abuse issues and recovery only

b. Substance abuse issues and health issues

c. Substance abuse issues and co-occurring disorders

d. All of the above

118. In a client's efforts to maintain emotional and psychological balance, what does the term *bookend* refer to?

a. Discussing a trigger event with someone trusted before and after it occurs

b. Fully reading and applying reference literature provided in the program

c. Remaining steadfast even in the face of temptation to abuse a substance

d. Keeping a difficult issue on the shelf until it can be better dealt with

119. In working with substance-abusing clients, counselors must be aware of the applicable guidelines in CFR Title 42 Part 2. What do the guidelines deal with?

a. Substance abuse treatment program accreditation and standards

b. Issues involving the illicit manufacture and sale of drugs of abuse

c. Confidentiality in areas of alcohol and substance abuse

d. Mandated client treatment under a court directive or order

120. In working with substance abuse clients, counselors must be aware specific guidelines found in the HIPAA statutes. What do these guidelines address?

    a. HIV counseling and practice guidelines
    b. Health privacy and confidentiality standards
    c. Health, addiction, and abuse practice guidelines
    d. Facility intake and admission policy standards

121. Confidentiality is particularly stringent in situations of alcohol abuse, drug abuse, and HIV infection. When are limited confidentiality breaches permitted?

    a. In situations where an individual is at real risk of harming him- or herself or others
    b. In situations of suspected child abuse and (in some states) in situations of suspected elder abuse
    c. Neither A nor B
    d. Both A and B

122. Group work is utilized extensively in substance abuse treatment. How do group therapy and 12-step groups compare?

    a. Very different types of groups with very different purposes
    b. Somewhat different group types with modestly different purposes
    c. Inherently similar groups, though with some different purposes
    d. Different names for the same groups with the same purposes

123. There are five primary group models used in substance abuse treatment. Which is the model that views dependency as a learned behavior that can be modified?

    a. Psychoeducational group type
    b. Cognitive-behavioral group type
    c. Interpersonal process group type
    d. Support group type

124. Matching clients with groups requires careful consideration. Where would a first-generation American Hispanic woman be BEST assigned?

    a. An all-women's group
    b. An all-Hispanic, Spanish-speaking group
    c. A group based on immediate needs
    d. A mixed new-immigrant group

125. Treatment for longer periods of time is closely associated with enhanced outcomes. What is the baseline duration for improved outcomes?

    a. Three months
    b. Six months
    c. Twelve months
    d. Eighteen months

126. There are numerous classification systems describing various stages of recovery. However, how many stages does the most common stage classification provide for?

    a. Three stages
    b. Four stages
    c. Six stages
    d. Eight stages

18

127. Beyond the five basic therapeutic group models (psychoed
behavioral, interpersonal, and support), other unique group m
specific, expressive, and relapse prevention. What does an expre
involve?

a. Communication skill-building education
b. Art, dance, and psychodrama therapies
c. Addressing distorted thinking and self-talk
d. Confrontational dialectic therapy

128. In 1965, Bruce Tuckman proposed a model of group developi
phases. What is the one phase that is NOT part of Tuckman's mode

a. Performing
b. Storming
c. Framing
d. Norming

129. A productive group therapeutic engages deep issues in many individuals with remedial
or neglected issues. This may at times induce regression. How is regression defined?

a. Feelings of regret and guilt that accompany past failures
b. A sense of emotional closure when painful issues are recalled
c. Reverting to a prior developmental level (i.e., juvenile or infantile)
d. Strong feelings of anger projected inward toward oneself

130. Substance abuse affects not only the user but the family as well. What are
intergenerational affects MOST commonly caused by?

a. The legal system, with incarceration, unemployment, and family separation
b. Compensating issues needed to cope with addictive dysfunction
c. The counseling system, pushing families to encounter an addict's issues
d. Society, rejecting the addict and all those associated with him or her

131. HIV remains a profound problem in the United States. What approximate percentage of
all HIV cases are found among females in this country?

a. 5 percent
b. 15 percent
c. 25 percent
d. 35 percent

132. Members of the lesbian, gay, bisexual, and transgender (LGBT) community face many
challenges, including issues of discrimination. Regarding substance abuse as compared with
the general population, how is the LGBT community likely to act?

a. Less likely to use alcohol or drugs
b. About as likely to use alcohol or drugs
c. More likely to use alcohol or drugs
d. Insufficient data to make these comparisons

most individuals with cognitive and physical disabilities desire to work, many
to do so. In consequence, as related to substance abuse and the general
on, how is this population likely to act?

a. More likely to use alcohol or drugs
b. About as likely to use alcohol or drugs
c. Less likely to use alcohol or drugs
d. Insufficient data to make these comparisons

134. The number of older adults is rapidly increasing in the United States and worldwide. As a group, when receiving appropriate treatment for substance abuse, how are older adults likely to act?

a. Less likely to continue to use alcohol or drugs
b. About as likely to continue to use alcohol or drugs
c. More likely to continue to use alcohol or drugs
d. Insufficient data to make these comparisons

135. The likelihood of developing a substance abuse disorder fluctuates throughout the life course. What is the most likely period in life for a substance abuse problem to begin?

a. Middle age
b. Young adulthood
c. Adolescence
d. Childhood

136. Research reveals that science-validated community and school prevention programs do work. Which of the following is NOT a category of youth prevention substance abuse programs?

a. Universal programs
b. Selective programs
c. Indicated programs
d. Targeted programs

137. Proper program and progress documentation is necessary for a great variety of reasons. Which of the following is NOT a particularly important reason?

a. Ensuring treatment plan accuracy and continuity
b. Avoiding client challenges of records and documentation
c. Ensuring compliance and continued agency funding
d. Avoiding loss or even retroactive return of funds

138. Accurate documentation and reports are necessary if effective treatment and recovery plans are to be developed and implemented. Which of the following is NOT fundamental assessment information at intake?

a. Documentation regarding referrals and referral outcomes
b. Psychoactive substance abuse history and patterns of use
c. Psychological health and psychiatric treatment history
d. Current physiological health and medical history

20

139. Treatment and recovery plans must remain current and effective for optimal client progress and well-being. Consequently, how often are treatment plans typically updated?

a. Every fourteen to twenty-one days or as changes or progress indicate a need
b. Every twenty-one to thirty-six days or as changes or progress indicate a need
c. Every thirty to ninety days or as changes or progress indicate a need
d. Every sixty to one hundred twenty days or as changes or progress indicate a need

140. What is the key difference between a current treatment plan and a current progress note?

a. The treatment plan evaluates client achievements, while a progress note ensures action steps are taken to meet objectives.
b. The treatment plan assesses client needs, while a progress note coordinates service providers' interventions.
c. The treatment plan records events and activities, while a progress note captures the client's current clinical presentation.
d. The treatment plan provides an action blueprint, while the progress note captures what did or did not occur.

141. Accurate records are the basis for the treatment plan and measuring client progress. If something is entered in a client record in error, what is the proper response?

a. Line through the error, writing *error* and initialing and dating the change
b. White-out or otherwise obscure the error to fully eliminate it from the chart
c. Remove the erroneous page and recopy all correct information onto a new page
d. Black out the error using a felt pen to ensure the error cannot be read

142. Clients actively in a treatment program need regular chart entries. Typically, state requirements mandate an updating entry no less often than

a. daily.
b. semi-weekly.
c. weekly.
d. monthly.

143. If a client leaves a treatment program early or involuntarily, how is the written discharge summary affected?

a. It is not needed altogether.
b. It is produced as usual.
c It is abbreviated or cursory.
d. It is comprised only of the terminal facts.

144. The Code of Federal Regulations, Title 42, Part 2, addresses client confidentiality. Other than through a written information release, when do exceptions to confidentiality exist?

a. When program funding requires it
b. When a police officer demands it
c. When a subpoena requests it
d. None of the above

21

145. The Code of Federal Regulations, Title 42, Part 2, Subpart E, addresses situations where law enforcement or courts can breach client confidentiality. What is a subpoena signed by a judge?

a. Sufficient for release of information, provided it is delivered by a law officer
b. Sufficient for information release, if signed by a federal court judge
c. Insufficient for information release, unless signed by two qualified judges
d. Insufficient, unless a qualified hearing is first held in court

146. Clients with an extensive substance abuse history often struggle with impulse control and anger. If a client becomes verbally agitated, angry, and elevated with a counselor, what is the BEST response?

a. Threaten to call law enforcement unless he or she calms down.
b. Cite the right to expel him or her from treatment if he or she misbehaves.
c. Validate his or her affect but not expression (if threatening)
d. Ignore the behavior so as not to further escalate his or her emotions

147. Many substance-abusing clients suffer from high impulsivity. If a client begins to act out inappropriately, what is an IDEAL grounding technique?

a. Verbal confrontation
b. Anchoring exercises
c. Walking out of the session
d. Pointing out program rules

148. Clients with a history of abuse have a tendency to place themselves in situations in which further abuse is likely, particularly an unsafe relationship. If this occurs, what is the counselor's BEST response?

a. Coach them to explore the situation, issues of risk, and self-endangerment.
b. Point out to them the issues that are obvious to the counselor.
c. Provide a lecture on issues of abuse recovery and important safety concerns.
d. Contact the unsafe individual, and intervene on the client's behalf.

149. A counselor finds herself treating a perpetrator of incest abuse. A survivor of past abuse herself, the counselor finds this deeply disturbing. What would be her BEST response?

a. Ignore her personal feelings, and focus on the client's issues and needs.
b. Confront the client about his past, and press for growth in this area.
c. Refer the client to a counselor more comfortable with the client.
d. Find a therapist to help her better cope with a client such as this.

150. In providing services, an agency needs to maintain a vision of purpose and important objectives. Of the following, what is the MOST significant mission?

a. To ensure the survival and funding of the agency to continue offering services
b. To ensure that staff have jobs so that they may continue offering services
c. To earn a reputation of stability and consistency in offering services
d. To break the cycle of abuse and neglect and its negative impact on others

Answers and Explanations

1. D: The DSM lists a set of eleven symptoms, 2 or more of which must have occurred at any time during the past 12 months for a diagnosis of substance use disorder. 1) Tolerance, defined as either the need for larger and larger amounts of the drug in question over time to achieve the desired result, or a decrease in the effect of the drug with continued use of the same amount 2) Withdrawal, defined by either the known withdrawal symptoms for a particular drug, or by the fact that the drug, or a similar drug, is taken to avoid withdrawal symptoms 3) An increase in the amount of the drug taken, or the continued use of the drug past the intended time 4) An inability to control usage 5) A large amount of time and effort devoted to obtaining the drug in question, using the drug in question, or recovering from its effects 6) The giving up of important activities in order to obtain or use the drug in question, or recover from its effects 7) The continued use of the drug in question regardless of the ill effects it has caused. 8) Craving 9) Recurrent drug use which leads to inability to fulfill major role 10) Recurrent drug use though it is physically harmful 11) Recurrent drug use despite it leading to continued social problems. He does not meet the criteria for current intoxication either. Recreational use commonly occurs biweekly or weekly, and the use is typically for reasons of sociality. Substance abuse counseling is therefore not indicated. However, counseling regarding the potential for life circumstances, stressors, or other unexpected losses or burdens to precipitate a future substance abuse problem should be discussed.

2. D: The amount of a drug ingested will typically affect the user's experience, with higher doses often producing a greater effect (though potentially diminishing over time as tolerance develops). The modality of administration can greatly influence the rate of the drug's uptake into the system. Normally the rate of effect, from greatest to least, is: inhalation (snorting or smoking), injection (intravenous, intramuscular, or subcutaneous), and ingestion (sublingual or swallowing with or without food). Generally, the faster the systemic uptake, the shorter and more intense the high experienced. Polydrug abuse greatly complicates the drug experience, particularly if the drugs used are chemical antagonists (e.g., stimulants and depressants—such as meth and alcohol), additive (producing a cumulative effect), synergistic (more than cumulative), or potentiating (each enhancing each other). The setting in which the substance use occurs is also often a significant contributor to the experience. The feelings engendered by the surroundings, the people with whom the experience is shared, the attitudes and reactions of others involved, as well as personal past drug experiences and individual biology all combine to produce a drug experience.

3. D: When a drug is used regularly, the body is gradually able to adapt to the effects of the drug. Evidence of tolerance is twofold: (1) greater doses of the drug are required to achieve previous effects, and (2) doses that would have produced profound physiological compromise or even death are now readily tolerated without untoward effects. In some cases, it has been noted that up to ten times a lethal dosage, or even more, may be taken without any signs of significant physiological compromise. Tolerance develops as the body seeks homeostasis, or a functional state of equilibrium, in spite of the presence of the drug.

4. D: Intense drug euphoria produces extremely intense, emotionally imprinted memory engrams, coupled with long-term changes in the amygdala area of the brain, which operate outside of conscious control. Key euphoric memories become integrally connected to sights, sounds, smells, people, and places previously associated with drug use. The reappearance of any of these past drug cues will often effectively trigger intense, amygdala-driven cravings for a drug. Cravings are further intensified by lingering imbalances in brain metabolism patterns, receptor availability, hormone levels, and other hypothalamus and pituitary-mediated sensations of dysphoria and distress. The cascading nature of these effects frequently induces a drug-use relapse.

5. C: While tolerance for barbiturates does develop, tolerance for an otherwise lethal dose only marginally increases and never exceeds twofold. This means that the likelihood of an unintentional fatal dose increases substantially over time as the need for the intoxicating effect pushes that threshold ever closer to a lethal dose. Given the impairments in memory and judgment that typically accompany CNS depressant intoxication, simple forgetfulness can lead to a fatal overdose. Finally, using barbiturates with any other CNS depressant substance, such as alcohol, can result in an additive CNS depression that can readily be fatal. Death most often occurs via respiratory or cardiac suppression.

6. D: Other symptoms of Wernicke's encephalopathy include poor muscle coordination and oculomotor impairment (problems moving the eyes in a controlled fashion). Wernicke's syndrome is a short-term condition resulting from vitamin B1 (thiamine) deficiency, typically developing after years of drinking and poor nutrition. Of those with Wernicke's syndrome, 80 to 90 percent will develop long-term psychosis and memory problems known as Korsakoff syndrome. While poor coordination is a symptom, retrograde amnesia (loss of old memories) and learning impairments are among the more classic hallmarks of the condition. Because they are so often found together, the two syndromes are often referred to concurrently as Wernicke–Korsakoff syndrome.

7. B: Hepatitis refers to inflammation of the liver. Alcohol is toxic to all body tissues. Because alcohol must be metabolized by the liver, it is particularly susceptible to the toxic effects. Consequently, many heavy drinkers suffer from alcoholic hepatitis, characterized by abdominal pain, nausea, vomiting, and a swollen liver. In more extreme cases, jaundice and bleeding can result. Jaundice (a yellowing of the skin and whites of the eyes) is from bilirubin, a by-product of aging red blood cells broken down in the liver, that should have been fully metabolized by the liver. Spontaneous bleeding occurs because key clotting factors are made in the liver, but production is inhibited by hepatitis. Steatosis consists of fatty deposits in the liver that, if severe, can prove fatal. Cirrhosis refers to scarring of the liver from alcohol damage, preventing its normal functioning. High blood toxins can also cause hepatic encephalopathy—a reversible dementia—if the toxins are reduced.

8. C: Chronic users of cocaine, crack cocaine, methamphetamine, and other such stimulants develop a profoundly unpleasant sensation of bugs crawling under their skin. They may even come to believe the bugs are present and needing to be removed. In less severe cases, users may pick at their skin to the point of causing sores and scabs. In more extreme cases, users may cut themselves in a desperate attempt to release the bugs and find relief. The condition is also known as Magnon's syndrome and may also be referred to colloquially as coke bugs or crank bugs, and so on.

9. D: Considerable medical research demonstrates that cocaine not only causes arterial constriction secondary to the drug's stimulant effects, but it also causes a cumulative effect, with more cocaine causing increased arterial narrowing. Atherosclerosis (artery hardening and plaque buildup) greatly magnifies this deleterious process. The result is that permanent disability or death due to sudden cardiac arrest or hemorrhagic cerebral stroke is an increasingly real possibility the longer the drug is abused. Finally, cocaine-induced damage to the prefrontal lobes (where behaviors are modified and controlled) often results in impaired judgment, disinhibition, loss of foresight, decisional incapacity, and chronic unpredictability and irritability.

10. B: Amphetamines consist of a group of synthetic stimulants chemically similar to the body's natural adrenaline—the hormone released when the body reacts in high-threat fight–fright–flight

24

circumstances. The three main types are: amphetamine sulphate (commonly known as speed or by its trade name, Benzedrine), dextroamphetamine (trade name Dexedrine or colloquially as Dexy's midnight runners), and methamphetamine (Methedrine or meth, crank, speed, poor man's cocaine, etc.). Among the three classes, methamphetamine has the greatest abuse risk due to its extremely intense rush. While some drugs such as heroin may be unpleasant at first use, amphetamines are immediately pleasurable to most users. Consequently, meth is second only to marijuana as the nonalcoholic drug most abused worldwide.

11. D: In terms of difficulty quitting, relapse rates, cravings ratings, and persistent use despite known harm, nicotine is substantially more dependency producing than cocaine, heroin, and alcohol. In terms of withdrawal symptom severity, nicotine exceeds that of cocaine and is only slightly behind heroin. Thus, fewer than 7 percent of those trying to quit each year will succeed. Given that nicotine use greatly increases the risks of heart disease, stroke, lung diseases, and cancer, nicotine abuse is a serious public health issue. Even only occasional smoking produces lung and vascular damage, and almost one-fifth of all heart disease deaths are linked to smoking.

12. D: Historically, the level of delta9-tetrahydrocannabinol (THC) in domestic U.S. marijuana was less than 0.5 percent. Recent cultivation and cross-breeding practices, however, have changed this, and some domestic marijuana has substantially higher levels. The THC in Mexican marijuana can range as high as 4 percent, and sinsemilla can reach concentrations as high as 8 percent. The potency of hashish (cannabis plant resin) can be as great as 10 percent, and hashish oil may contain as much as 20 percent THC. Street marijuana products may be diluted or cut with other adulterants (oregano, catnip, etc.) and may also be laced with other undisclosed psychoactive ingredients such as opium or LSD. Unexpectedly high doses of THC or the addition of other psychoactive substances can greatly affect the unsuspecting user in potentially troubling ways. Thus, caution is in order.

13. A: Convergence theory postulates that substance abuse rates are becoming more equal during the twenty-first century—currently, 1.6 men have substance abuse issues for every 1 woman with such issues. Others, however, suggest the data is flawed, as women are more likely to hide their substance abuse behavior and less likely to see help. Other gender differences include the following: (1) men externalize accountability, women internalize (self-blame); (2) issues of self-esteem are more common for women; (3) treatment barriers are higher, as women tend to have pregnancy issues and children needing their care; (4) women tend to increase substance abuse when depressed, while men are more likely to decrease use. Women prostitute to support a habit; men turn to selling drugs or other criminal behavior. Marriage is a deterrent to drug use for men but a risk factor for women. Women drinkers are four times more likely to live with a drinker than is a man.

14. D: Alcohol use disorders rank third among psychiatric disorders of the elderly. Some 2 to 4 percent of the elderly have a substance use disorder (including alcohol, drugs, or both). Approximately 15 percent of the elderly with an alcohol disorder will also have a concurrent drug abuse problem. Due to physical changes of age, researchers recommend only one drink per day as the upper limit. Detecting alcohol and drug abuse in the elderly can be difficult as the symptoms are often very similar to other health problems associated with age. Isolation, poor health, pain, or depression often motivates substance abuse in the elderly. Many are ashamed of the abuse and further avoid family and others to hide the problem. Suicide rates climb as people grow elderly, and 25 to 50 percent of all attempts by the elderly involve alcohol. Some 10 percent of the elderly misuse their prescription medication, intentionally or accidentally. Substance abuse may greatly complicate a potentially tenuous status for many on complex medication regimens.

15. D: Early-onset alcoholism refers to an onset of alcohol abuse in adolescence or young adult life. This represents about two-thirds of all individuals with an alcohol use disorder. Late-onset exacerbation drinking refers to individuals with an intermittent history of alcohol abuse that only became chronic in late adulthood. Late-onset alcoholism refers to individuals with no prior life history of alcohol abuse who developed an alcohol problem solely in later life. This category of alcoholism may be more amenable to treatment than the earlier-onset forms. Detoxification can be protracted in the elderly, requiring a longer treatment stay, due to the metabolic changes of aging. Group treatment can be complicated by the group milieu, where younger participants may leave the elderly feeling estranged and out of sync with the other participants. Careful efforts at inclusion or an alternate group composed of older participants may be required.

16. A: Exploring readiness for change, rules and expectations, or issues of confidentiality may otherwise serve only to induce client anxiety, defensiveness, or rejection of potential treatment outright. The counselor must generate an authentic and safe environment that is conducive to trust and disclosure. This can be achieved, from a motivational perspective, by assuring the client that he or she will not be told what to do, but rather, help will be given in deciding what he or she is seeking to accomplish. A direct request about what has brought the client in can be helpful if they are ready to talk openly. Otherwise, asking about health, work, or family challenges may provide an oblique entry to asking about substance issues (e.g., "How is this affected by your substance abuse?"). As rapport grows, issues of confidentiality, program requirements (e.g., whether or not sessions can be held in spite of intoxication, etc.), session length, evaluation of change readiness, and so on, can then more naturally unfold.

17. D: The goal of motivational interviewing is to help the client discover his or her own desire to change. Thus, confrontation, stern accountability, overt reality testing, and other coercive or argument-inducing approaches are avoided. Five fundamental principles to guide the motivational interviewing process are: (1) reflective and empathetic listening, (2) identification of variances between behavior and personal goals, (3) deflection of confrontation or argument to more positive, goal-oriented dialogue, (4) redirection of client resistance to desires and goals rather than opposing it outright, and (5) nurturing optimism and a sense of self-efficacy when confronted with obstacles, challenges, and negative expressions.

18. A: According to the 2009 National Survey on Drug Use and Health, when individuals have co-occurring disorders (dual diagnoses) consisting of substance abuse and mental illness, only 7.4 percent will receive treatment for both disorders, 32.9 percent will receive only mental health treatment, and 3.8 percent will receive only substance abuse treatment. Where mental illness is severe, the existence of a substance abuse problem is particularly likely (25.7 percent). And among individuals with a substance use disorder in the past year, 17.6 percent will have a concurrent mental illness disorder. Thus, where either a substance abuse disorder or a mental illness disorder is known to exist, treatment professionals should be particularly careful to screen further and ensure that any coexisting disorder is identified, if one exists.

19. D: Experienced counselors and researchers are aware that the setting in which screening occurs (home, office, clinic, or voluntary vs. involuntary facility) can significantly affect the results of any screening tool used. How instructions are given can substantially influence the findings as poorly chosen words and presenting attitudes can unquestionably taint client thinking, presumptions, and willingness to disclose. The presence or absence of privacy can also be a significant factor, as distractions, fears of disclosures or being overheard, and other such elements can bias and the screening and intake process. Further, the levels of rapport and trust between the client and the intake counselor may also alter client perceptions and, consequently, client responses during any screening interview or when completing any screening instrument. New counselors must, therefore, be alert to these factors and quickly learn to overcome any deleterious influences.

20. C: Certified Alcohol and Drug Abuse Counselors, absent additional mental health training and licensure, do not have the credentials and training necessary to diagnose mental disorders. They do have the training and certification necessary to diagnose substance abuse disorders and are well within their scope of practice to screen, assess, and otherwise evaluate clients for substance abuse issues and to formulate and carry out substance abuse treatment plans. Because of the frequency with which co-occurring mental illnesses exist within the substance abusing community, Certified Alcohol and Drug Abuse Counselors can become very familiar and proficient with numerous commonly occurring mental disorders. It can therefore seem natural to broaden the scope of practice as experience grows. However, legal scope-of-practice parameters do not provide for Certified Alcohol and Drug Abuse Counselors to diagnose mental illness, and it is essential that they collaborate with other professionals whenever non-substance abuse mental health issues arise.

21. A: GATE was established by a consensus panel addressing the evaluation of suicidal ideation and behaviors by substance abuse counselors working with at-risk clients. It consists of activities that are well within the practice scope of a substance abuse counselor. Gathering information involves (1) screening for suicidality and (2) observing for warning signs. Screening involves direct questions regarding current thoughts (plans, means, or preparations) and any past history of attempts. Accessing supervision or consultation (even if the counselor already has specialized training) ensures issues of risk are fully evaluated. Taking responsible action protects client well-being and safety. Extending the action involves securing follow-up and ongoing monitoring as needed. In this way, GATE fully assesses and addresses suicidality. The final step is thorough documentation to secure a medical and legal record of the care provided.

22. A: Political orientation is not typically a sensitive issue in the assessment process. Comprehensive assessment domains include: (1) complete substance abuse history (all substances past and recently used, modes of use, frequency and amounts, etc.); (2) full addiction treatment history (when, where, how long, etc.); (3) significant physical and mental health history (including medications and ongoing care needs, suicidality, etc.); (4) familial history and current issues (marital status, family supports, etc.); (5) educational history; (6) employment history (and current issues); (7) legal or criminal history (including any ongoing matters such as pending court, probation, parole, etc.); (8) emotional, psychological, and perceptual concerns (worldview issues); (9) spiritual or religious issues; (10) lifestyle concerns (sexual orientation, housing transience, etc.); (11) socioeconomic factors (finances, work benefits, insurance, etc.); (12) prior community resource use; (13) cognitive capacity and behavioral functioning; (14) readiness for treatment.

23. C: Serious mental health issues, such as persistent suicidality, delusions, or hallucinations that precipitously resolve with abstinence are most likely substance abuse-induced disorders that will not reoccur without a return to the former substance abuse. In like manner, serious mental health issues that do not resolve in an abstinence period of thirty days or longer are likely due to an underlying mental disorder that must be evaluated and properly treated. In certain circumstances, an underlying mental disorder becomes exacerbated by substance abuse. In these situations, some measure of improvement will be noted, but it will fall substantially short of total resolution. This reflects the persistence of the underlying disorder; they will still need appropriate treatment for meaningful resolution of the condition.

24. B: This instrument was designed specifically for use with adolescents, drawing upon situations that are common to this age group. The instrument derives its name from the key word in each of the screening questions: driving a car while intoxicated; using alcohol or drugs to relax, feel better, or fit in; using alcohol or drug when alone; forgetting events that occurred while using alcohol or drugs; requests by family or friends to limit use; and, getting into trouble while using alcohol or drugs. The other instruments are: AUDIT (Alcohol Use Disorders Identification Test); the CAGE (also an acronym: needing to cut down drinking, feeling annoyed at drinking criticism, feeling guilty at drinking, and needing a morning eye-opener drink); and, the MAST (Michigan Alcoholism Screening Test).

25. C: It is important to introduce the topic rather than simply launching into questions. In this way, the client can understand for the questions that follow. This introduction should be followed by very clear questions. Screen for thoughts: "Have you had thoughts about deliberately ending your life?" Screen for past attempts: "Have you ever tried to end your life?" A past history of attempts greatly increases the likelihood of future attempts. Any affirmative response to thoughts should lead to questions such as: "Have you had these thoughts for long?" "What have you been thinking of doing?" "Have you made firm plans about this?" "Do you have (the pills, etc.) that you've been thinking of using?" Where a client has begun to formulate clear plans and realistic means, and so on, immediate intervention is essential.

26. D: The purpose of screening is to methodically review a client's presenting circumstances by which to determine the appropriateness (or lack thereof) for placement or referral for further assessment and evaluation. Screening tools are also used to identify the presence or absence of co-occurring disorders, particularly those that might contribute to substance abuse. Screening tools do not attempt to diagnose a presenting co-occurring disorder but rather to establish the likelihood that one may be present. Where a client presents as potentially having a significant co-occurring disorder, the client is then referred to the proper clinician (psychologist, psychiatric social worker, psychiatrist, etc.) for further evaluation and diagnosis. Once a diagnosis is obtained, a treatment plan can be formulated that addresses the co-occurring disorder as well.

27. D: The primary purpose of substance abuse assessment is to develop a full understanding of the severity and extent of a substance user's drug or alcohol abuse problem. However, the assessment process should also identify and explore other closely related issues such as co-occurring disorders (both mental and physical), significant others, employment and education, finances, and other social and legal concerns. The overarching goal of assessment is to gather sufficient information to establish (1) a working diagnosis of current substance abuse, (2) significant co-occurring disorders, (3) the quality and availability of important supports, (4) readiness for change, and (5) all other necessary information sufficient to establish a meaningful and successful treatment plan.

28. B: Client collaboration in treatment planning is essential as client buy-in is essential to ultimate success. While various generic treatment plans may be useful in ensuring that all essential elements of planning have been addressed, boilerplate plans should not be used to short-cut the planning process. The inclusion of the client's most important personal goals may well be crucial to the buy-in required. The outcome should be a written document that includes: (1) treatment goals, (2) action steps that are both measurable and time sensitive, (3) clearly defined expected outcomes, and (4) explicit verbal or even written agreement between the counselor and client.

29. B: Careful assessment documentation, information sharing, and summarizing with the client for feedback can help ensure that the assessment information is accurate and readily available. However, to be most effective, assessment information must be converted into clear goals, objectives, and action steps. Beyond this, the assessment must be recorded in a clinically useful, reliable, and valid manner. In this way, the information and data can be readily understood and replicated and applied in a uniform manner most relevant to treatment. Simplistic labels, unidimensional scores, and checklists will not alone achieve these ends. The record must include adequately organized narration and summation to be fully effective.

30. D: Clients are largely unaware of the consultations that treatment team members engage in throughout the treatment process. However, an awareness of the benefits of treatment—not only for the issue of substance abuse or alcohol but for other related life concerns—can substantially increase a client's commitment to a treatment program. In like manner, the client needs to fully understand the treatment process. In this way, the purpose and goals of interventions can be clear, and motivation to adhere to treatment consequently increases. Finally, fully assuming the patient role is important because, in this way, the client resolves to put him- or herself completely into the hands of treatment provides. A relinquishment of this nature removes attitude and behavioral barriers and results in more effective treatment functioning.

31. B: The American Society of Addiction Medicine (ASAM) recognizes four levels of treatment placement and five specific levels of care. The lowest level (referred to as Level 0.5) is designated as early intervention, which refers to education and other services for individuals with at-risk behaviors but for whom a substance abuse diagnosis cannot be confirmed. Level I consists of basic nonresidential outpatient services, primarily education, counseling, and behavioral change. Level II offers Intensive outpatient or partial hospitalization (inpatient evenings or weekends, etc.). The focus is on comprehensive biopsychosocial assessments and individualized treatment plans. Level III consists of residential or inpatient treatment and offers a planned regimen of care in a twenty-four-hour live-in setting. Level IV is medically managed intensive inpatient treatment. Level IV provides twenty-four-hour medically directed evaluation and treatment of substance-related and mental disorders in an acute care setting.

32. C: In assessing clients, the American Society of Addiction Medicine (ASAM) encourages evaluations using six interactive dimensions: (1) acute intoxication or withdrawal potential (the level of intoxication or risk of severe withdrawal symptoms or seizures and exploring inpatient or ambulatory detoxification); (2) biomedical conditions and complications (other illnesses that may create risk or complicate treatment); (3) emotional, behavioral or cognitive conditions and complications (diagnosable mental disorders or mild, undiagnosable mental problems that complicate treatment); (4) readiness to change (open or resisting treatment, acknowledging or denying addiction, high or low motivations, etc.); (5) relapse, continued use or continued problem potential (immediate or low risk of substance use; good or poor coping or relapse prevention skills; severity of collateral problems such as suicidal behavior; etc.); (6) recovery environment (influence or proximity of people, resources, and situations that may help or pose a threat to safety or continued treatment).

33. A: Individual drug use patterns over the lifespan. Lifespan research suggests that all behaviors, including drug use, have multiple origins, changes, and transitions arising from related biological, psychological, and social contributions. For that reason, drug use research extends from embryological genetics, through the development of personality, and on through the life course in terms of related sociocultural and psychological influences, changes in use through aging, etc. An individual's pattern of use throughout the lifespan may be referred to as his or her "drug trajectory" and use pattern. Recent advances in genetics research have aided in better understanding how genes vs family origin contribute to the decision to use illicit drugs and how addiction may subsequently develop.

34. A: CMRS scales, by G. De Leon, were developed to aid in determining client readiness for substance abuse treatment. The scales measure client perceptions in four interrelated domains: circumstances (the external pressures influencing substance abuse change), motivation (internal pressures driving change), readiness (perception and acceptance of the need for treatment), and suitability (the client's perception of the appropriateness of the treatment modality or setting) for community or residential treatment. CMRS scales consist of eighteen Likert-type (five-point, strongly disagree to strongly agree) response items. The scores are summed to derive a total score. Research on validity and reliability has offered strong support for the CMRS scales.

35. D: External events and pressures may persuade or even compel a client to enter treatment, and treatment admission may follow. However, true readiness is when a client perceives and then accepts the need for treatment. This typically requires the client to possess at least some insight into his or her condition, the associated costs and consequences, and a recognition that self-induced efforts have been unsuccessful. Finally, readiness involves a meaningful desire to effect change. The use of assessment instruments, such as the use of circumstances, motivation, readiness, and suitability scales can be particularly helpful in judging readiness for change.

36. B: This acronym represents the following guiding treatment planning principles: M = measurable. Goals and objectives must be clearly measurable so that progress and other changes can be identified readily and documented. A = attainable. Goals and objectives, and interventions as well, must be achievable (attainable) during the active treatment phase. T = time limited. The active focus of treatment should be on short-term or time-limited goals and objectives. R = realistic. It must be realistic for a client to complete the identified objectives of each goal within the specified time period. S = specific. Objectives, and associated interventions, must be sufficiently specific and goal focused to ensure progress toward attainment. A key element is involving the client directly in the planning process to ensure that the goals, objectives, and action steps are mutually derived to ensure client buy-in and commitment.

37. C: Treatment may be begun during incarceration, continued at transfer to minimum security, then to a halfway house, and finally out to home on probation or parole. At all transition points, treatment plans should be updated. This need is particularly acute because an offender's level of treatment needs, due to potential problems with motivation and environmental stressors, may significantly change at each of these junctures. Case management is typically required to ensure comprehensive services, and common participants include criminal justice staff, prerelease planners, halfway house staff, vocational or educational staff, health providers, and involved family. Because of the frequency of co-occurring disorders in this population, numerous professionals use the Integrated Screening, Assessment, and Treatment Planning model as it provides for evaluation of both substance abuse and mental health issues.

38. A: The Addiction Severity Index (ASI) addresses six problem domains: (1) medical status, (2) employment and supports, (3) alcohol and drug use, (4) legal status, (5) family and social status, and (6) psychiatric status. At times, alcohol and drug abuse are separated, resulting in a total of seven domains. It is important, however, to emphasize that the ASI is not a comprehensive instrument. For example, it does not ask questions regarding pregnancy or homelessness, for example, even though either of these issues may be of crucial importance to the client. The ASI was designed to primarily explore issues of addiction and other common, closely related issues. The goal of the ASI is to produce a standardized baseline, ensuring that all counselors consistently ask the basic questions (an important construct of research reliability in data gathering). Additional questions may need to be asked to ensure that the client's needs are fully understood and incorporated into any forthcoming treatment plan.

39. C: The Addiction Severity Index (ASI) was first released in 1977 and formally adopted for use by the National Institute on Drug Abuse in 1980. The ASI was developed by the Drug Evaluation Network Systems, which was sponsored in this endeavor by the White House Office of National

Drug Control Policy (ONDCP) and the Center for Substance Abuse Treatment (CSAT). Since that time, the ASI has become the most widely used assessment instrument in the field of addictions. It is recommended as a baseline instrument for addiction assessment by a great many governmental and private substance abuse treatment organizations, and due to its standardized questions, it is particularly useful for research. A teen version (T-ASI) and a shortened version (ASI-Lite) are also available. Currently in its fifth iteration, version six is in development.

40. D: Reliability addresses how well an instrument consistently gives accurate information. Accuracy is of little value if the aspects or issues being measured are not those the instrument was intended to measure. In like manner, an instrument that accurately addresses the intended aspects or issues is still of little value if the measurements taken by it are inaccurate. Thus, to be truly useful and effective, assessment instruments and tools must be both reliable and valid. In multiple studies, the Addiction Severity Index has been proven both reliable and valid.

41. A: Drugs of abuse are not able to successfully treat depression. While transient relief can be experienced, the subsequent withdrawal depression invariably serves to worsen the original symptoms. Among the most common assessment tools for depression is the twenty-one-item Beck Depression Inventory, now in its second revision (BDI-II). The BDI is designed for use with individuals between the ages of thirteen and eighty. It can be utilized as a self-report instrument, or administration may be provided by a verbally trained administrator. The new format is inclusive of a prior two-week period, and other items were revised to assess both increases and decreases in sleep and appetite, better allowing formulation of a DSM diagnosis.

42. C: Clients may enter treatment by court order or family pressure. Motivation for behavioral change is a personal and internal matter, with a greater likelihood of ultimate success. Assessing motivation may be pursued via the Stages of Change Readiness and Treatment Eagerness Scale (SOCRATES). It is a nineteen-item self-report instrument comprised of three main scales—recognition, ambivalence, and taking Steps—requiring approximately three minutes to complete. SOCRATES identifies client states on a continuum between not prepared to change and already changing. Those in the pre-contemplation stage typically deny the problem. Clients in the preparation and action stages typically admit that they have a problem. Optimal treatment planning requires an understanding of where a client is in the change readiness process, which also promotes more effective exploration of the current barriers to further change. There are two versions of SOCRATES. One version is used to assess alcohol issues and the other addresses personal drug use.

43. D: The key components of a treatment plan include: (1) problem statements, which are based on information obtained during the assessment; (2) goal statements, which are derived from the problem statements; (3) objectives, which consist of what the client will do to meet treatment goals; and (4) interventions, which are defined as what the staff will do to assist the client. Relevant client strengths are often a required component. It is often useful to draw problems from a master problem list. The list should include all identified problems, regardless of available program services, and whether they should be immediately addressed or deferred. Identification of problems is a shared client–counselor endeavor. Problem statements should be nonjudgmental, jargon-free, and written in complete sentences. Couch problem statements in behavioral specifics to ease writing goals, objectives, and interventions.

44. B: The SOAP note was first generated by Dr. Lawrence Weed, MD, in the 1970s to provide physicians with rigor, structure, and a way for practices to communicate with each other. *Subjective* provides a narrative summary of the client's current condition, usually including the presenting problem (why they came to be seen). Common elements include: (1) onset (if applicable); (2)

chronology (improvements or worsening, variations in the problem, etc.); (3) symptom qualities (the nature of the symptoms, etc.); (4) severity (degrees of distress); (5) modifying factors (what helps or worsens the condition, etc.); (6) additional symptoms (whether related or unrelated to the presenting problem); and (7) treatments (prior treatments, if the client has previously been seen elsewhere). *Objective* captures key facts that are measurable, quantifiable, and repeatable aspects of the client's situation (physical symptoms, lab results, weight, etc.). *Assessment* refers to the clinician's early diagnostic impressions. *Plan* describes the clinician's next steps in response to the information obtained (further assessments, referrals, medications, interventions, etc.).

45. D: DAP notes assist clinicians record clear and organized notes to better understand client thinking, select appropriate goals, and track client progress. The data section includes facts such as client statements, observations regarding mood and behavior, past assignment reviews, and so on. This section is typically the longest portion of a DAP note. The assessment section includes client current status and evaluation of treatment progress. It may also include tentative or working diagnoses, potential treatment requirements, and information regarding a client's motivation or ability to proceed. The plan section includes session scheduling and the expected focus for upcoming treatment sessions. In this area, updates or alterations in treatment are recorded, along with comments regarding homework assignments. DAP notes allow others to understand events during each therapy session and evolutions in treatment and can aid in tracking long-term progress and program and intervention effectiveness in a consistent manner.

46. D: The acronym DIG-FAST is a tool prompting the full evaluation of the symptoms of mania. Each letter addresses one of the key potential features of mania: distractibility (easily distracted as evidenced by an inability to concentrate), indiscretion (excessive pleasure activities), grandiosity (larger-than-life feelings of superiority, wealth, power, etc., often experienced during manic, hypomanic or mixed episodes), flights of ideas (mind is racing, seemingly unable to control or slow down thoughts), activity (markedly increased activity, with weight loss and increased libido), sleep deficit (unable to sleep for extended periods well below normal sleep needs but not drug induced), talkativeness (pressured speech: rapid, virtually nonstop, often loud and emphatic, seemingly driven, and usually hard to interrupt).

47. C: The Center for Substance Abuse Treatment (CSAT)—part of the Substance Abuse and Mental Health Services Administration within the U.S. Department of Health and Human Services—notes that substance abuse has been treated as an acute disorder for most of the twentieth century. This shaped treatment, which was typically short term and intensive, much like treating an acute infection. Detoxification occurred, information was shared, and the individual was discharged to manage independently. They now recommend that substance abuse be treated like a chronic condition, such as diabetes or hypertension. To this end, treatment needs to be realigned to allow for a gradual recovery with regular checkups to ensure that the condition remains in control.

48. B: In keeping with the chronicity model of treatment (suggesting that substance abuse treatment requires a long-term treatment model, much like a chronic illness) as opposed to the acute treatment model, the Center for Substance Abuse Treatment (CSAT) recommends that treatments or other care provided following program discharge be referred to as continuing care. Thus, the terms *aftercare* and *follow-up care* are to be discouraged. In this way, care provider models can better perceive the need to realign themselves from an acute care model to a chronic care model. The result is expected to be better and more enduring care and support for those working to overcome issues of addiction and compulsion. Examples of continuing care include mutual-help groups (including twelve-step and other support groups) available in the community and follow-up client appointments for episodic checkups, similar to typical medical checkups for other chronic diseases).

49. D: The policy of the American Medical Association (AMA) is that clients coping with substance abuse disorders should receive formal treatment from qualified professionals. Mutual-help groups may provide adjunctive services and may be a part of a successful treatment plan. The American Psychiatric Association (APA), the American Academy of Addiction Psychiatry (AAAP), and the American Society of Addiction Medicine (ASAM) have concurred, asserting in a joint policy statement that treatment involves at least: (1) a qualified professional providing services; (2) a thorough evaluation to determine the severity and stage of the illness and to screen for other mental and medical disorders; (3) a properly developed treatment plan; (4) that the treating professional or program remains accountable for the treatment and additional service referrals as necessary; (5) that the treatment professional or program remains in contact with the client until the recovery process is complete. While mutual-help groups are important, they cannot substitute for professional treatment.

50. C: Intensive outpatient treatment (IOT) has traditionally consisted of a minimum of nine hours of weekly treatment provided in three three-hour sessions. However, some programs provide more contact hours and others as few as six contact hours per week. Even so, according to the American Society of Addiction Medicine (ASAM)'s Patient Placement Criteria, IOT programs must provide nine or more structured contact hours each week and treatment at six or more hours per day during a partial hospitalization program. The Center for Substance Abuse Treatment (CSAT) consensus panel agreed that IOT key features include: (1) six to thirty contact hours each week; (2) step-up and step-down care with varying intensity; (3) a minimum of ninety days continuing care following discharge; and (4) various additional core features and services.

51. D: Recreational therapy was not one of the core features and services referenced by the Center for Substance Abuse Treatment (CSAT). The CAST consensus panel agreed that intensive outpatient treatment (IOT) core features and services must include the following: intake and orientation; full biopsychosocial assessment; individualized treatment planning; individual, family, and group counseling; psychoeducational programming; case management; linkages with mutual-help and community-based support groups; twenty-four-hour crisis support; medical treatment; formal drug screening and monitoring (urine or breath tests); educational and vocational services; psychiatric evaluation and psychotherapy; medication management; and discharge planning and transition (discharge) services. They further defined potential enhanced services to include: adult education; recreational activities; housing and food resources, smoking cessation treatment; transportation referrals; child care; and parenting skills education.

52. C: Naltrexone is effective for some people with alcohol dependency. It has also been noted, however, that naltrexone may not be effective in treating men with chronic, severe alcohol dependence. In certain circumstances, naltrexone has also been effective in treating opioids addiction. Disulfiram (Antabuse) is another adjunctive medication used in the treatment of alcoholism. Naloxone (Narcan), a shorter-acting agent similar to naltrexone, is used primarily in situations of opioid overdose, though it is also used in the treatment of alcoholism to lower cravings. Buprenorphine and buprenorphine combined with naloxone are now also available for the treatment of opioid dependence and can be prescribed in programs that have medical personnel on staff.

53. C: Although exercise can be an important stress reducer, and health improvement is also meaningful, these are not core treatment and recovery skills. Substance refusal training is crucial as development of this skill helps clients to practice and become comfortable with refusing addictive substances. Outside of the program, it is inevitable that clients will at times be offered illicit substances, and they need the skills to reflexively but politely refuse without returning to substance abuse. Stress management and relaxation training are both important as unmanaged stress is a significant trigger for relapse. Assertiveness training teaches individuals how to get their needs met proactively (but not aggressively) and to avoid allowing others to take advantage of them. Unmet needs can be a powerful trigger to relapse, thus this is an important skill.

54. A: Gustatory refers to the sense of taste and is not a learning style. To learn, we utilize our senses to process information around us. When learning, most people use one of their senses more than the others. There are actually seven learning styles: (1) aural (auditory–musical): learning through sound; (2) visual (spatial): learning via images; (3) verbal (linguistic): learning through words; (4) physical (kinesthetic): learning via touch; (5) logical (mathematical): learning through logic; (6) social (interpersonal): learning best with others; (7) solitary (intrapersonal): learning through self-study. The three most common learning styles are visual, auditory, and kinesthetic. Consequently, programs should explore the use of videotapes, behavioral rehearsals or role plays, written materials, lectures, discussions, workbook assignments, and daily logs or journals. In this way, all primary learning modes can be met.

55. C: It has been noted that substance abuse treatment outcomes can be substantially improved when supportive family members are involved. However, it is also true that problematic family relationships can greatly hamper the treatment process and reduce the likelihood of enduring recovery. This is particularly true where family culture and traditions run counter to treatment and recovery processes. Ideally, family therapy will be available as an adjunct to the treatment process, as necessary. Where program resources lack this component of care, referrals to therapists or organizations that provide family therapy should be considered. Involved family members will also need to be educated regarding the addiction process as well as learning how to optimally support their loved one's recovery. Balance is important as attempts to exert too much control can drive their loved one away or even back into abuse. Conversely, where family involvement is too limited, the client may lack the support necessary to sustain themselves into recovery and beyond.

56. C: The five main levels in the substance abuse continuum of care, as identified by the American Society of Addiction Medicine (ASAM) are: Level 0.5: early intervention services (subclinical or pretreatment, exploring risks and addressing problems or risk factors that appear to be related to substance use); Level I: outpatient services (nonresidential, less than nine hours per week); Level II: intensive outpatient or partial hospitalization services— nonresidential, a minimum of nine hours per week (Level II is subdivided into levels II.1 and II.5); Level III: residential or inpatient services—minimum of twenty-five hours per week (Level III is subdivided into levels III.1, III.3, III.5, and III.7); and Level IV: medically managed intensive inpatient services (subacute, with daily physician supervision). These levels are not discrete but rather points on a treatment continuum.

57. B: Independent of the levels of care defined by the American Society of Addiction Medicine (ASAM), outpatient clients must work through four sequential stages of treatment, regardless of the entry treatment level of care. The stages consist of: Stage 1—treatment engagement (establish a treatment contract including goals and client responsibilities; resolve acute crises; develop a therapeutic alliance; and prepare a treatment plan); Stage 2—early recovery (continue abstinence; sustain behavioral changes; terminate a drug-using lifestyle and develop drug-free alternatives; learn relapse triggers and prevention strategies; identify and resolve contributing personal problems; and begin a twelve-step or mutual-help program); Stage 3—maintenance (solidify abstinence; deepen relapse prevention skills; enhance emotional functioning; increase sober social networks; and address other problem areas); Stage 4—community support (sustain abstinence and a healthy lifestyle; establish treatment independence; extend social network and support group connections; pursue healthy community activities; and solidify important outlet activities and pursue new interests).

58. C: The most common recommended minimum duration of days in an intensive outpatient treatment (IOT) phase is ninety days. However, research reveals that longer duration of care is related to better treatment outcomes—specifically, less substance use and better social functioning in clients over time. Consequently, it may be both advantageous and cost-effective to plan lower-intensity outpatient treatment over a longer time period to enhance treatment outcomes. The ultimate duration should be adjusted to meet the client's rate of progress, psychiatric status, support system, clinical needs, and so on. IOT programming is commonly provided for nine or more hours over three to five days per week. The consensus panel recommends six to thirty hours, depending upon client needs. For some clients, more frequent, shorter visits may be of greater benefit than fewer, longer sessions. For other clients, more or longer sessions, approaching the intensity of partial hospitalization, may be needed.

59. D: Research reveals that the effectiveness of group therapy is on a par with that of individual therapy. In addition, group therapy allows for a more effective balance of costly individual counseling services. Intensive outpatient treatment (IOT, Level II care) is typically delivered in sequential stages, with greater service intensity and structure gradually reduced as clients progress. This allows for increasing personal responsibility even as structure and staff supervision is reduced. However, it is important to be able to return to more intensive services if changing client circumstances require it. The sequenced nature of IOT can motivate clients toward recovery milestones and stage completion criteria. Celebrating or otherwise marking the transition between IOT stages can provide further motivation. Finally, complex information can be better delivered via sequenced stages as this allows for conceptual units that are more easily understood and that can be revised to meet the unique cognitive, psychological, and transition readiness of each client.

60. D: Psychoeducational groups teach key concepts regarding substance use disorder and its consequences. Time-limited, these groups are ideal for education at the outset of treatment. The low-key educational nature (as opposed to emotionally intense therapy groups) allows more objective examination of dysfunctional beliefs, problem thinking patterns, along with relapse prevention and skills training. Skills-development groups focus on refusal training, relapse prevention, assertiveness training, and stress management. Support groups address immediate issues along with ways to change negative thinking, emotions, and behavior, learning new ways of relating, managing conflict without violence or relapse, and evaluating how actions affect others. Interpersonal process groups include single-interest groups (focused on specialized issues, usually later in treatment) and family or couples groups that explore the effects of substance use on relationships.

61. B: Individual counseling is typically scheduled for thirty to fifty minutes at least weekly in the initial treatment stage. Sessions are held with a primary counselor to help facilitate a meaningful, collaborative therapeutic alliance. A common session format involves: (1) asking for reactions to recent group meetings; (2) reviewing outside activities since the last session; (3) asking about current feelings; (4) exploring any interim drug and alcohol use; and (5) inquiring about any urgent issues. Recent group topics, treatment plans, and coping strategies are reviewed. Fears and anxieties about change are explored, and drug testing feedback is provided. Sensitive issues not appropriate for the group are discussed. However, no effort is made to address any underlying conscious and subconscious issues contributing to substance use. Assistance with access to needed services outside the program's scope is given, and planning for transitions between levels of care or for discharge is completed. The session concludes with a review of the client's plans and treatment schedule. Clients with co-occurring disorders may require primarily individual counseling.

62. D: Pharmacotherapy and medication management are of critical importance in effective substance abuse treatment. They must not be overlooked or isolated from other therapies and

35

interventions. Even so, medications cannot alter lifestyles or recover the functional damage that results from drug abuse. Due to the three- to five-day weekly schedules of most intensive outpatient treatment (IOT) programs, they are an ideal setting for identifying medication needs and then initiating and monitoring the necessary medications. IOT program-based pharmacotherapy and medication management can facilitate: (1) ambulatory detoxification; (2) withdrawal symptom relief; (3) craving reduction; (4) blocking the reinforcing effects of drugs; (5) reducing the health risks that accompany the use or injection of illicit drugs; (6) mitigation of certain underlying psychopathologies that may predispose substance abuse or relapse; (7) the monitoring and treatment of numerous potential medical conditions that may result from acute or long-standing substance abuse.

63. A: Substance abuse and recovery topics addressed in psychoeducational groups are presented in a sequential, building order of concepts to ensure optimum learning. Core topics include: (1) understanding the relapse process; (2) relapse prevention tools; (3) creating a personal relapse plan; (4) managing euphoria and desires to test control; (5) stress management and coping skills; (6) anger management and relaxation techniques; (7) self-efficacy in relapse-risk situations; (8) managing slips and avoiding escalation; (9) recovery resources; (10) structuring leisure and recreation; (11) essentials of personal health; (12) regular personal inventory; (13) managing emotional triggers (shame, guilt, depression, and anxiety); (14) problem family dynamics (enabling and sabotaging); (15) restoring personal relationships; (16) healthy sexuality; (17) essential educational and vocational skills; (18) essential living skills (financial management, housing, and legal assistance); (19) finding meaning in life (spirituality); (20) grief and loss and substance use; (21) parenting essentials (children's needs, developmental stages, and tasks); (22) maintaining balance in life.

64. C: The Clinical Institute Withdrawal Assessment–Alcohol, Revised (CIWA-Ar) scale assists in identifying which alcohol-dependent clients can receive ambulatory detoxification versus inpatient care. The CIWA-Ar can be administered in minutes by staff with a minimum of three hours training. There is some disagreement about cutoff points on the scale. Numerous physicians concur that scores of twenty or higher should be treated in a medical inpatient setting. Other specialists suggest that clients with scores into the low twenties can be safely managed in an outpatient setting, providing there is proper monitoring, medications supervision, and so on. Consequently, medical staff must rely on their best judgment or program policy and procedures. The CIWA-Ar also guides the administration of medications at thirty- to sixty-minute intervals. Doses are only given in response to observed withdrawal signs at a specified intensity. The CIWA-Ar has reduced both client numbers receiving medications and the amounts of medications given. Revisions of the instrument have enabled the monitoring of both benzodiazepine and opioid withdrawal symptoms.

65. C: There are effective medications for the treatment of alcohol and opioid addictions. The medications reduce cravings, inhibit the intoxicating effects, produce aversion, and lessen the desire to use the target substance. However, in spite of considerable laboratory research and extensive clinical trials, no effective medications for the treatment of dependence on stimulants such as cocaine, marijuana, inhalants, or hallucinogens has been discovered. There are medications to modestly mitigate the difficult withdrawal symptoms caused by these substances. For example, symptoms of stimulant withdrawal include insomnia, agitation, anxiety, and even delirium, psychosis, and hyperthermia in particularly acute cases. Neuroleptic medications can lessen the symptoms of psychosis and delirium, and benzodiazepines can reduce the symptoms of agitation and anxiety. Beyond symptom management, however, there are no target treatment drugs for these substances.

66. A: Education, vocational training, and employment issues are core support concerns but do not constitute adjunctive therapies. Adjunctive therapies are used to enhance the emotional and psychological functioning of clients laboring to overcome an addiction. Given the pressures of foregoing their substance of choice, individuals in recovery need alternative outlets for stress as well as better self-care skills. To this end, creative media groups (e.g., dance, drama, music, crafts, and arts) can be very therapeutic and helpful in the recovery process. Other alternative therapies include acupuncture and biofeedback therapy. Both of these can aid in reducing stress and in learning relaxation skills. Similarly, a variety of meditation techniques can be particularly helpful.

Mediation techniques include approaches such as mindfulness (learning to appreciate the present), visualization (positive imagery), breath meditation (learning to focus and control thinking and the body), and transcendental meditation (deep awareness and consciousness). As an adjunct to substance abuse treatment, meditation is in harmony with the intent and philosophy of twelve-step and other mutual self-help groups.

67. C: The majority of drug- or alcohol-dependent individuals are also smokers. And, more in this group die from smoking-related conditions than from their substance abuse. Treating staff believe that smoking cessation may complicate drug or alcohol abstinence. However, clients may feel otherwise—believing the best time to quit would be during treatment for their drug or alcohol use. Fewer than 10 percent of clients would object to a clinic's smoking ban if nicotine replacement therapy was available. Smoking cessation success is highest when coupled with behavioral therapy and nicotine replacement therapy. Thus, treatment programs are ideal settings for smoking cessation. Finally, there are strong associations between reduced smoking and reductions in substance abuse. Numerous forms of nicotine replacement are available, and clients are encouraged to try various products before deciding what works best for them. The antidepressant medications bupropion and nortriptyline help to reduce nicotine cravings, probably because they help reduce depression—which is a major cause of relapse.

68. D: Disulfiram (Antabuse) is indicated even with cocaine use or methadone maintenance. Disulfiram interferes with acetaldehyde metabolism, which produces a profound physical reaction if drinking occurs within twelve hours to seven days, depending on dose. The reaction involves facial flushing, followed by a throbbing headache, tachycardia, tachypnea, and sweating. Some thirty to sixty minutes later, nausea and vomiting occur, often accompanied by hypotension, dizziness, fainting, and collapse. The full cycle takes one to three hours. Careful blood alcohol monitoring is needed to ensure that no alcohol is present before administering disulfiram. Low doses (125 mg) can be given as quickly as the blood alcohol reaches zero. An initial dose of 250 to 500 mg may be used, though lower doses may be better for small women, the elderly, and those with liver impairment. Clients have taken the drug as long as sixteen years. Episodic use is effective to guard against drinking in high-risk situations (e.g., special events or celebrations, etc.). Food that contains alcohol usually does not cause a problem if it has been evaporated during the cooking process.

69. B: Optimizing the intake process enhances the likelihood that the client will both disclose crucial intake information and accept treatment. Overly formal intake questioning is likely to be off-putting and may well inhibit self-disclosure and engagement. Both research and anecdotal evidence suggest that less-formal approaches can better build and support rapport between the counselor and client. One less formal approach is the sandwich technique. It involves sandwiching the standard screening and assessment questions between two less-formal discussions. For fifteen to thirty minutes, the counselor: (1) addresses perceptions of the problems that motivated the client to explore treatment; (2) elicits the client's expectations of treatment; (3) supports the commitment to change; (4) offers encouragement that change can be achieved; and (5) explores readiness to change. Next, the formal screening and assessment are conducted, followed by: (1) a less-formal summarizing of findings; (2) initial treatment planning appropriate to the client's change stage; and (3) addressing the individual's expectations for treatment.

70. C: Researchers have compared eight commonly used screening instruments for efficacy in determining the presence of substance use disorders. Only three possessed optimal accuracy, positive predictive value, diagnostic sensitivity. These three instruments are: (1) the Center for Substance Abuse Treatment (CSAT) Simple Screening Instrument; (2) the combined Alcohol Dependence Scale (ADS) and the Addiction Severity Index (ASI)-Drug Use Subscale; and (3) the Texas Christian University Drug Screen. Other popular brief screening instruments include the Substance Abuse Screening Instrument, the CAGE Questionnaire, and the Offender Profile Index. Each of these instruments is in the public domain and thus may be reproduced and used freely.

71. C: The Substance Dependence Severity Scale (SDSS) is a structured interview that provides current (last thirty days) DSM and ICD-10 substance use disorders and harmful use diagnoses. The instrument measures the quantity and frequency of recent drug use, which directly translates into variations in clients' clinical status. Following the usual two to three days of training (for those with a preexisting clinical assessment and diagnosis background), the SDSS can be administered in thirty to forty-five minutes. Past research indicates that the SDSS dependence scales are reliable and valid measures of DSM diagnostic severity. More recent investigations into test–retest reliabilities for the ICD-10 dependence scales yielded good to excellent results for alcohol, cannabis, cocaine, and heroin. Test–retest reliabilities for the ICD-10 harmful use scales fell in the good range for alcohol, cocaine, and heroin but were poor to fair for cannabis. Concurrent validity, diagnostic concordance, and internal consistency results were similar to the test–retest findings. These findings support the use of the SDSS in assessing DSM and ICD-10 dependence and harmful use diagnoses.

72. A: The Texas Christian University Drug Screen (TCUDS) scale is able to distinguish between individuals with drug use disorders as opposed to those who misuse drugs but are not physically and psychologically dependent. The TCUDS instrument consists of twenty-five questions administered in less than five minutes. The TCUDS is frequently used in adult criminal justice settings. However, it is also appropriate for use in the general population. The TCU Drug Screen II (TCUDS II) is a standardized fifteen-item screening tool also designed to identify any current history of heavy drug use or dependency. Items on the TCUDS II are designed to meet the criteria found in the Diagnostic and Statistical Manual (DSM) and the NIMH Diagnostic Interview Schedule (NIMH DISC). The scale is divided into two parts, with the first assessing drug and alcohol use problems and the second addressing frequency of use and the individual's readiness for treatment. The TCUDS II can be used in an interview setting, or it can be self-administered.

73. B: Physiological dependence exists if tolerance or withdrawal is in evidence. Tolerance is in evidence if there is a need for significantly more of the involved substance to achieve a desired effect or intoxication or if the effects of the substance are significantly diminished when the same amount of the substance is used. Withdrawal is in evidence if abstinence induces a withdrawal syndrome as expected for the substance or the same substance (or one closely related chemically) is used to relieve or ward off withdrawal symptoms. The DSM lists a set of eleven symptoms, 2 or more of which must have occurred at any time during the past 12 months for a diagnosis of substance use disorder. 1) Tolerance, defined as either the need for larger and larger amounts of the drug in question over time to achieve the desired result, or a decrease in the effect of the drug with continued use of the same amount; 2) Withdrawal, defined by either the known withdrawal symptoms for a particular drug, or by the fact that the drug, or a similar drug, is taken to avoid withdrawal symptoms; 3) An increase in the amount of the drug taken, or the continued use of the drug past the intended time; 4) An inability to control usage; 5) A large amount of time and effort devoted to obtaining the drug in question, using the drug in question, or recovering from its effects; 6) The giving up of important activities in order to obtain or use the drug in question, or recover from its effects; 7) The continued use of the drug in question regardless of the ill effects it has caused; 8) Craving; 9) Recurrent drug use which leads to inability to fulful major role; 10) Recurrent drug use though it is physically harmful; 11) Recurrent drug use despite it leading to continued social problems

74. C: Early. Early remission is no stimulant use criteria being met (except for craving) for at least 3 but less than 12 months. Sustained remission is no stimulant use criteria being met (except for cravings) for 12 months or longer. The terms full and partial are no longer used to describe remission.

75. D: The family of origin refers to blood relationships (parents, siblings, cousins, grandparents, etc.). The relationships in both family types are important in substance abuse treatment. Either group may bring factors and influences that contribute to substance abuse (e.g., alcoholism, culture or traditions supportive of drug experimentation, etc.). Where outright drug or alcohol use was not condoned, families may have interactive patterns that predispose substance abuse. Troubled families often have too few or too rigid rules, difficulties with intimacy, and ineffective problem solving. Such families often perpetuate a don't-trust-don't feel-don't-talk paradigm that allows isolation, damaging alliances, enmeshment, or other dysfunctions to persist. It is essential for counselors to learn about both the positive and negative resources in a client's family. Referrals for family counseling may be essential to this end. When the family becomes ready to change negative behaviors and adopt new, healthier ones, they become supporters in the treatment process.

76. D: Dual relationships are unethical during and immediately following the course of any counselor–counselee relationship. More broadly, dual relationships arise when multiple roles are created outside the therapeutic–fiduciary relationship. Examples include: (1) allowing a client to provide automobile repair work for a therapist, whether it is paid or not; (2) hiring a client to paint a therapist's home; (3) allowing a client to provide volunteer clerical work in the program office; and so on. Multiple roles such as these compromise the integrity of the therapeutic process, making it more difficult to provide client services that are untainted by the ancillary roles. Working through difficult issues becomes highly problematic—is it really about the issue at hand or the quality or willingness with which the ancillary role is carried out? Termination, closure, referrals, and so on all become laden and troublesome.

77. C: A substantial gift may be loosely defined as one exceeding $20 in value. The giving of small gifts is not uncommon, and these gifts are usually acceptable—particularly if they can be shared by all staff or clients. At times, gifts may also be culturally significant, and extra care may be needed to ensure no offense occurs. These are often handmade items or items representative of a culture, ethnicity, or home country. Many will have unique meanings and background stories. Certain cultures view gift giving as a demonstration of respect and gratitude for a valuable service. Failure to accept could result in termination of treatment. Such gifts should be accepted whenever possible. They are not typically given with any ulterior motives. Inappropriate gifts (e.g., those that are too personal, too costly, or offered in exchange for favors, etc.) should be tactfully and politely refused. Citing program rules can help to explain and prevent problems. All gifts should be reported to supervising staff and entered into the case record.

78. A: Most treatment programs have policies that prevent clients from engaging in intimate relationships that might undermine treatment. This typically includes prohibiting clients and counselors from socializing outside the confines of the program. Some programs also discourage any contact between clients outside the program's structured activities. Virtually all programs discourage dating, sexual relationships, moving in together, and other forms of significant involvement. However, many programs do encourage clients to collaborate in mutual-help group attendance, and some even encourage mutual support in other meaningful aspects of their lives. Where boundary issues occur, options include assigning one of the clients to another group or providing individual counseling to one while waiting for the other to complete the program. Should mutual substance abuse occur, recommitment contracts and renewed abstinence contracts may be needed. Regardless, it is important for counselors to fully understand the boundaries within the treatment program and to consistently apply these guidelines.

79. C: No effort should be made to engage the client in such a public setting. Remaining at the club would likely precipitate some sort of contact. Therefore, leaving without contact would be best. Then, later, when the client returns to the program, a private conversation should be engaged. During this discussion, the client can be informed of the unexpected contact and what was witnessed. In this way, the client is able to privately disclose his or her issues regarding the lapse (or relapse, as the case may be) with regard to the return to using alcohol. This discussion can then build to include those issues, experiences, and triggers that may have contributed to the occurrence. In this way, the client can use the experience to build upon those skills needed to increase his or her abstinence goals and the steps needed to achieve them.

80. D: Many substance abuse counselors have a past history of substance use and thus also hold membership in mutual-help programs. Where a client from a treatment program is encountered in a mutual-help setting, it is essential for a counselor to maintain appropriate boundaries between these separate roles (professional vs. consumer). To this end, it would not be proper for a counselor to become a client's sponsor. To minimize potential conflicts, counselors should not attend meetings where current or former clients attend. Where this cannot be avoided, the counselor should not share his or her personal issues at that meeting. If a counselor needs to talk, he or she should share with other non-clients privately after a meeting or contact his or her sponsor. To prevent such dilemmas, some cities host counselor-only meetings. These are typically not listed in the general mutual-help directories. To locate a mutual-help program of this composition, a counselor should contact the intergroup office or consult with other counselors in the area.

81. B: Research is unable to confirm any optimal counseling approach as numerous factors, such as the substances used, degrees of dependency, treatment duration, irregular client characteristics, and so on, will inevitably shape research outcomes. Further, clients typically have complex psychosocial needs and unique personal and emotional factors that will require considerable creativity by involved providers. Consequently, counselors increasingly use a variety of approaches that are revised and tailored to meet each client's singular needs. This kind of theoretical accommodation and modification is a hallmark of effective treatment. However, when altering or combining approaches, counselors will need to recognize that theoretical conflicts may arise. In some cases, these conflicts could attenuate or even extinguish the success of the approach. Consequently, counselors must have a competent grasp of the approaches being utilized to ensure that ineffective or untoward outcomes are not unintentionally produced.

82. D: Using a modified Minnesota Model of treatment (i.e., first used at Hazelden Foundation and Willmar State Hospital in Minnesota in the late 1940s), twelve-step facilitation, involves a thorough introduction to twelve-step principles, education about the disease of alcoholism (or other drugs), and strong encouragement toward participation in twelve-step groups. Twelve-step fellowships, such as Alcoholics Anonymous (AA), are guided by the philosophy that alcoholism (or other addiction) is a progressive disease with psychological, biological, and spiritual aspects. The twelve-step approach gradually evolved for use with drug addictions and various compulsive disorders (e.g., eating disorders). Treatment programs that use twelve-step facilitation teach twelve-step principles, begin working the twelve steps, achieve abstinence, and move clients to community-based twelve-Step groups (e.g., AA, Cocaine Anonymous [CA] or Narcotics Anonymous [NA]). In these programs, educational efforts present alcoholism as a disease marked by denial and loss of control. Outside work includes reading twelve-step materials, journal writing, and other personal recovery-oriented tasks.

83. C: Twelve-step programs offer easy monitoring of assigned step tasks. Among the many benefits of twelve-step program participation are: (1) cost—meetings are a free, available virtually worldwide, and they provide a source of continuous support; (2) many larger cities offer specialized meetings for those with unique needs (e.g., youth, women, specific sexual orientations, treatment beginners, foreign language speakers, etc.); (3) the twelve-step approach addresses recovery in varied domains, such as cognitive health, spiritual health, and physical health realms, accommodating a focus of almost any potential participant; (4) the twelve-step approach easily accommodates clients from diverse ethnic, cultural, and other backgrounds. These benefits make the twelve-step approach uniquely beneficial as an important adjunct to comprehensive treatment. Primary drawbacks include: (1) it is difficult to accurately monitor client compliance with step tasks or even meeting attendance; (2) the emphasis on a higher power may be problematic for some clients; (3) smaller communities may not be able to sustain ongoing twelve-step meetings, issue-specific groups, or meetings well suited to dual-diagnosed (psychiatric disordered) clients.

84. A: Clients are less likely to feel pressure to attend twelve-step groups by staff very familiar with the twelve-step approach. Rather, they are more likely to feel they receive useful encouragement and support from these staff persons. To ensure adequate familiarity, staff (particularly those with no past experience receiving substance abuse treatment) are encouraged to: (1) read Alcoholics Anonymous (AA), Narcotics Anonymous (NA), Cocaine Anonymous (CA), and other twelve-step program literature; (2) frequently attend open twelve-step meetings; (3) attend a diversity of twelve-step groups to better identify the unique milieu of those programs available (especially groups that are open to clients with co-occurring psychiatric disorders); and (4) study thoughtfully to ensure that they deeply understand the beliefs, values, and mores that undergird the twelve-step fellowships. In this way, staff can be particularly supportive and directive as clients explore the twelve-step approach to recovery and ongoing abstinence.

85. C: The three approaches all produced positive outcomes in improving drinking from admission baseline to one year in follow-up. However, twelve-step facilitation showed a measurable advantage when clients were followed for three years post treatment. Other studies have comparatively investigated the outcomes of aftercare by way of structured relapse prevention and twelve-step facilitation. Of importance, the twelve-step facilitation approach has provided more positive overall outcomes for the greater share of people who abuse substances. The findings were particularly positive for: (1) clients who were experiencing high levels of psychological distress; (2) substance users who were women; and (3) clients who reported the use of multiple substances at the outset of treatment. Specifically, these three groups clearly remained abstinent for more extensive periods following treatment with twelve-step facilitation, as compared to structured relapse prevention. In point of fact, both approaches have contributions to make to the recovery process. However, where limitations in resources, time, and other obstacles exist, it is particularly important to ensure that members of these three groups are meaningfully encouraged to participate in available twelve-step programs.

86. D: From the first therapeutic community (Synanon, founded in 1958 in California by Chuck Dederich), treatment communities (TCs) were organized as controlled, drug-free residential treatment settings providing intensive and comprehensive treatment. The central goal is to produce a holistically healthy lifestyle, engaging emotional, psychological, and social issues that may lead to

41

substance use. Residents learn from each other, staff members, and other authority figures. This has come to be referred to as community-as-method perspective, which sees the whole community (clients, staff, social structure, and daily activities) as the active therapeutic agent. Many early TCs utilized punitive contracts, privilege losses, and extreme peer pressure to produce change. The more harsh aspects have since been significantly modified, though peer pressure remains a key motivator. The TC model has been expanded to include additional services, such as mental health and medical services, educational and vocational services, and family education and therapy. Today, many TC programs are carried out in intensive outpatient treatment (IOT) programs, serving clients transitioning out of residential or incarceration settings or bypassing residential treatment altogether.

87. C: Rehabilitation refers to the recovery of skills and abilities that have been lost. Due to extended and severe drug use, criminal behavior, or co-occurring disorders, many therapeutic community (TC) clients need to develop skills and abilities they never previously properly possessed. The TC model views substance abuse as a holistic (whole person) disorder rather than as an isolated disorder. Consequently, TC clients are assessed across an interrelated continuum of psychological and social deficits (e.g., dishonesty, poor impulse control, anger issues, etc.), along with their substance abuse patterns. The key beliefs and values necessary for recovery include: (1) complete honesty; (2) reality orientation to the here and now; (3) personal accountability for all behavior; (4) empathy and concern for others; (5) a strong work ethic and realization that rewards must be earned; (6) proper differentiation between external behavior and the inner self; (7) understanding that change is always occurring; (8) understanding that learning has value; (9) developing economic self-sufficiency; (10) community involvement is important; and (11) quality citizenship matters.

88. D: Researchers investigating therapeutic community (TC) treatment have found that residential and day-only TC treatment program outcomes are not significantly different. Consequently, trends toward intensive outpatient treatment (IOT) using the TC treatment model should be effective. Studies funded by the National Institute on Drug Abuse (NIDA) have revealed that participation in TC treatment is correlated with measurably positive outcomes. For example, treatment outcome data from the longitudinal Drug Abuse Treatment Outcome Study found that completing TC treatment was associated with reduced use of alcohol, cocaine, and heroin, as well as reductions in depression, criminal behavior, and unemployment, as compared against levels experienced prior to treatment. Further, a study of inmates transitioned from an institutional TC program to a TC-oriented outpatient work-release program experienced lower rates of recidivism (re-incarceration) and drug use than those receiving institutional TC treatment alone. Thus, TC treatment appears to be an effective approach to reducing substance abuse, criminal activity, depression, and unemployment among individuals with positive criminal and drug use histories.

89. B: A key feature of therapeutic communities (TCs) is structured programming. This involves scheduled activities and routines that help clients learn to avoid chaotic lifestyles and focus on daily activities that prevent the boredom and negative thinking that so often accompanies relapse behavior. TC treatment protocols consist of phases and stages that allow the tracking of client activities and measurement of progress. Treatment duration is dependent upon successful client progress. Staff and peer networks offer support, and other community-based services are integrated as needed to sustain recovery. The TC treatment approach is ideal for clients with past criminal issues, educational and employment deficits, relationship problems, and a history of failed treatment. Because of the focused, hierarchical, and often confrontational features of this treatment modality, it must be modified for those with co-occurring psychiatric disorders, antisocial personality traits, and various other dysfunctional behaviors. When used in an intensive outpatient program, a drug-free environment must be ensured.

90. A: The Matrix Model (also referred to as neurobehavioral treatment) was formulated during the 1980s' spike in cocaine and methamphetamine abuse. The model utilizes a complementary set of evidence-based practices coordinated and delivered as a program. Drawing upon cognitive-behavioral therapy, motivational interviewing, and findings from relapse prevention literature, combined with educational support and twelve-step program involvement, the model seeks to coordinate and optimize evidence-based treatments and support resources. Guiding principles include: (1) developing a positive therapeutic relationship; (2) applying a scheduled structure and expectations; (3) educating participants and families regarding brain chemistry, cravings, recovery, and relapse prevention; (4) incorporating cognitive-behavioral concepts for change; (5) reinforcing positive behavioral changes; (6) outlining the expected course of treatment and recovery; (7) promoting self-help (twelve-step) participation; and (8) using regular drug testing (urinalyses) to track progress.

91. D: Considerable research has demonstrated that community reinforcement (CR) and contingency management (CM) are both independent-effect treatment interventions. Further research, however, does support that CR and CM are most effective when used in conjunction with each other. Because a return to baseline drug use can follow the termination of CM, in particular, more long-term supports (such as twelve-step program involvement) may be needed for more enduring success. Maximum benefits accrue with larger rewards that increase in value to maintain CM motivation. By contrast, CR typically involves rewards from more-enduring sources (family, job, pleasurable activities, etc.) that can more naturally persist after treatment completion. Even so, education in relationship enhancement, goal setting and attainment, balanced lifestyle, and so on, can more fully ensure long-term treatment benefits. Finally, rewards and other reinforcements must be consistently applied and must only be provided in response to measurable successes (e.g., extended negative-result urine screens, etc.).

92. D: The old view that one disorder should be stabilized before another can be treated has been found to be flawed. It is important to coordinate the treatment of co-occurring disorders as treatment may otherwise be counterproductive and otherwise ineffective. For example, many substance abuse treatments are confrontational, tightly scheduled, and semi-authoritarian in nature—particularly those programs for court-ordered clients. However, clients with psychiatric disorders may do very poorly in such treatment paradigms. Many suffer from depression, anxiety, paranoia, self-abuse (cutting, etc.), suicidal ideation, or personality disorders, among other possible symptomatology. Others struggle with fears about psychotropic medications to treat their co-occurring conditions and may also resist pharmacological treatment of their substance abuse. Clients struggling with such issues are far less likely to cope well with common substance abuse treatment approaches. Consequently, program adaptation and specialized staff training may be required.

93. C: Individuals admitted for substance abuse treatment who also have a co-occurring psychiatric disorder are more likely to be female alcohol abusers than female drug users or male users of either alcohol or drugs. While most drug abusers are referred for treatment through the criminal justice system, female alcohol users are most typically referred through health care providers. Multiple studies reveal that the rates of co-occurring disorders are roughly that about 39 percent admitted for substance abuse treatment programs will meet *Diagnostic and Statistical Manual* of Mental Disorders (DSM) criteria for antisocial personality disorder; 11.7 percent are suffering with major depression, and 3.7 percent are struggling with a general anxiety disorder. Other challenges common among clients with dual-diagnoses (co-occurring disorders) include: chronic

43

unemployment and homelessness, family conflict and disruption, incarceration and subsequent law enforcement involvement (probation or parole), and violent victimization. Further, complex problems such as suicidal ideation and attempts, medication noncompliance, high self-medication needs, emotional issues, significant medical problems, and a host of other challenges often complicate the treatment process.

94. B: The Substance Abuse and Mental Health Services Administration (SAMHSA) has offered a Service Coordination Framework for Co-Occurring Disorders, which offers four categories by which to indicate the level of care a given client needs: Category I—mental disorders, less severe + substance use disorders, less severe; locus of care is a primary health care setting; Category II—mental disorders, more severe + substance use disorders, less severe; locus of care is a mental health system; category III—mental disorders, less severe + substance use disorders, more severe; locus of care is a substance use treatment system; and Category IV—mental disorders, more severe + substance use disorders, more severe; locus of care is state hospitals, jails or prisons, emergency rooms, and so on. In the first category (low severity mental health and substance use), the bias is for basic primary care. The middle two categories involve a bias for treatment in concert with the severity level of the primary diagnosis. The last category recognizes that, when both psychiatric disturbances and drug use are severe, clients tend to need highly integrated, even locked, care settings.

95. A: Client information, immediate behaviors, current medications, family history, and so on may well be indicative of a co-occurring disorder. However, they are not definitive criteria. The diagnosis must be proven or validated by the client's ongoing clinical presentation. Symptoms of withdrawal, as well as those of acute or chronic alcohol and drug toxicity, can readily present as a psychiatric disorder. They can also mask underlying psychiatric symptoms. True psychiatric symptoms often become apparent during the early stages of abstinence. Program staff should recognize that co-occurring disorders are common. Beyond the client's clinical presentation, additional attention should be given to: (1) the psychiatric history of the client and his or her family, especially documented diagnoses, prior treatment, and any psychiatric hospitalizations; (2) medications and medication compliance; and (3) ongoing symptoms and mental status changes over time. As the assessment proceeds, caution must be taken to ensure the client is properly treated for any serious medical withdrawal problems. Other safety issues, such as suicidality or homicidality and any inability to function, communicate, or care for oneself also should be responded to aggressively.

96. A: The physical, emotional, and cognitive changes of this developmental period make treatment more complex. Physical changes are marked by rapid growth, hormonal fluctuations, and the development of secondary sex characteristics. Cognitively, attention spans are shorter, projected awareness of the future is poor, abstract thinking skills are inconsistent, and impulsivity is high. Ideals, morals, and values are still developing, and intellectual interests are expanding. Not until late adolescence do youth become substantially aware of the consequences of their actions, thus allowing meaningful goal setting. The onset of substance abuse in this population is frequently associated with family dysfunction, parental substance use, peer influence, and troubled personal choices. Genetic background and cognitive dysfunction may also play a role. Other risk factors include: (1) a history of personality problems, poor parental or guardian relationships, academic failure, family disruption, and past victimization. An adolescent treatment provider must successfully cope with developmental, behavioral, psychiatric, family, and other treatment challenges. Most will only superficially resemble the challenges of adult clients.

97. C: Family therapy posits that conditions leading to adolescent drug use began in the home, and thus, the family can help with recovery. Family-based therapeutic approaches include multidimensional family therapy and multisystemic therapy. These approaches extend classic family therapy models to promote change in four areas: (1) the adolescent, (2) family members, (3) family interaction patterns, and (4) outside (nonfamily) influences. The family cognitive-behavioral therapy approach combines family systems theory with cognitive-behavioral therapy. The premise is that family cues and contingencies reinforce the conditioned behavior of adolescent substance abuse. Adolescent community reinforcement focuses on altering environmental influences that perpetuate substance use while also teaching enhanced coping skills for better self-management. The family support network develops a support group for parents, augmented with group and home therapy sessions. The family intervention program focuses on the family and other systems that affect the family (e.g., schools and the community). It partners a family therapist with a community resource specialist to address key family issues that arise when an adolescent uses substances.

98. C: Culture is best understood broadly, referring to a shared set of values, norms, and beliefs common to any group of people, whether it is based on race, ethnicity, nationality, or any other shared identity or affiliation. According to 2010 Census Bureau figures cited by the Brookings Institute, approximately 12.9 percent of the current U.S. population is foreign born (of note, the figure exceeded 13 percent during every decade from 1860–1920). Beyond country of birth, however, there are many other variables that can shape a client's culture and worldview. Diverse client populations include: non-white Hispanics and Latinos; African Americans; Native Americans; Asian Americans and Pacific Islanders; persons with human immunodeficiency virus/acquired immunodeficiency syndrome (HIV/AIDS); lesbian, gay, bisexual, and transsexual (LGBT) populations; those with disabilities; rural populations; homeless populations; and older adults. Counselors must navigate between the prevailing culture, treatment culture, and the client's culture as coping styles, social supports, stigma, and a myriad of other factors can be profoundly influenced by a client's culture.

99. B: It is the provider who is primarily responsible to ensure that treatment is effective for clients of cultural diversity. Ensuring effective treatment requires two separate understandings: (1) how to properly communicate and interact with persons from differing cultures and (2) knowledge of the specific culture from of the person receiving service. In truth, every competent and caring clinician should always look past stereotypes, seek shared understandings, treat clients with respect, maintain an open mind, ask questions when needed (both of clients and other involved providers), and remain willing to learn. Thus, being culturally competent merely makes explicit this ongoing duty and obligation. Beyond this, however, providers should diligently endeavor to acquire a deeper and broader understanding of the major values, mores, standards, and expectations of those cultures he or she routinely serves—while still, however, allowing for idiosyncratic variations within that cultural paradigm. In this way, culturally diverse clients can receive effective, meaningful, and culturally acceptable services in a sensitive and kind way. Doing so ensures even greater treatment efficacy and more enduring positive outcomes.

100. C: The term *culture-bound syndrome* has been used in different ways. First, it can refer to an illness truly bound to a specific culture. For example, the mottled discoloration on the thighs caused by the heat of a laptop resting on the legs of an excessive techie computer user or the fatal brain disorder (kuru) caused by now-banned cannibalism among the South Foré people of the eastern New Guinea Highlands. Second, it can refer to otherwise common mental or physical illnesses that are subsequently construed as unusual because of the pathoplastic influence of culture. For example, interpreting the hallucinatory symptoms of schizophrenia as evidence of demonic possession or considering the apparently other worldly experience of grand mal seizures to be a sacred disease—as described by Hippocrates—and more recently by the animistic Hmong, who may then revere and elevate such persons to the station of shaman.

101. C: Not only do clients bring their culture to the treatment experience, but counselors do as well. A group of professionals also has a culture that consists of shared values, norms, and beliefs. Complicating the clinician's culture further is the language (jargon) used, an emphasis on books, the professional mind-set (way of looking at things), and so on. Health institutions and training facilities are grounded in Western medicine, launched in ancient Greece, emphasizing the central role the human body in disease. Further, objectivity and scientific and empirical methods are the only trusted source of knowledge about diseases and treatment. By 1900, Western medicine began to recognize social contributions to disease, widening the view to issues of diet, lifestyle, employment and income, and family structure, which led to the field of public health. These cultural views make it harder for counselors to recognize symptoms couched in non-Western medical language or to understand a client's concerns and needs. Finally, different assumptions about the clinician–client role model, the etiology of illness, and acceptable treatments offer further relational barriers.

102. C: Biological psychiatry is focused on the biological causes and treatments of psychiatric disorders. The first forms of biological psychiatry appeared in the mid-nineteenth century and paved the way for pharmacological therapy for mental illness. The practice of psychotherapy (or talk therapy) emerged near the end of the nineteenth century with the establishment of psychotherapy (originally psychoanalysis) by Sigmund Freud. Although numerous disparate forms of psychotherapy now exist, all emphasize verbal communication as the basis for treatment. Most modern approaches now combine pharmacological therapy and psychotherapy, referred to as multimodal therapy. However, the emphasis on verbal communication retains the potential for miscommunication and more especially so when counselor and client come from different cultures. Misunderstandings can result in misdiagnoses, treatment conflicts, and noncompliance. Thus, the importance of effective cross-cultural communication continues to assume greater significance.

103. D: Discrimination and racism limit recreational and leisure opportunities to improve mental health. While leisure and recreational activities are important to mental health, racism and other forms of discrimination are not typical sources of limiting these resources and opportunities. The terms *racism* and *discrimination* refer to attitudes, beliefs, and practices that prejudge and denigrate individuals or groups solely based on disparate phenotypic characteristics (e.g., skin color, hair texture, facial features, etc.) or ethnic minority group affiliation. Despite some improvements, racial discrimination continues and has been documented in the area of health care. Examples include fewer medical diagnostic and treatment procedures for African Americans as compared with whites, demeaning and belittling expressions, and less time and attention given to eliciting and addressing other health care needs. Racism and discrimination can be intentional or unintentional and can be perpetrated by individuals, groups, and institutions. Because racism and discrimination can be insidious and go unrecognized, it is crucial that it be continuously evaluated, especially in cross-cultural situations.

104. D: As recently as 1990, about 23 percent of adults were from ethnic and racial minority groups. By 2025, it is estimated that 40 percent of adults (and 48 percent of children) will be from these same groups. Even among the four most representative ethnic and racial minority groups, great diversity exists. For example, Asians and Pacific Islanders consist of at least forty-three distinct subgroups speaking more than one hundred different languages. Hispanics may be further divided into Central and South Americans, Cubans, Mexican, and Puerto Ricans, among many others. More than five hundred tribes fall under the heading of American Indian or Alaskan Natives, each with different ancestry, cultures, and languages. African Americans are also an increasingly diverse group as immigrants continue to arrive from Africa, the Caribbean, and South America. Degrees of acculturation and mainstream assimilation vary widely. Higher birth and immigration rates have resulted in a 56 percent increase in Hispanics—the fastest-growing minority group in the United States.

105. C: Human immunodeficiency virus HIV is the virus that causes the acquired immunodeficiency syndrome (AIDS) syndrome. HIV is the viral agent that causes AIDS, which is the final stage in the HIV disease process. The Centers for Disease Control and Prevention reports that more than 918,000 people have AIDS at any given time (2004). The disease continues to be most prevalent among men who have sex with men and intravenous drug users, with these groups collectively accounting for almost four-fifths of all cases of HIV/AIDS. The disease disproportionately affects minorities. While13 percent of the U.S. population is African American, they represented 50 percent of all new HIV infections in 2004. HIV is also spreading rapidly among women and adolescents, with nearly half of new HIV cases reported among females age thirteen to twenty-four, and more than 60 percent among females age thirteen to nineteen. Gay substance abusers are at high risk because they more frequently engage in high-risk sexual behaviors when intoxicated. Although new medications have significantly extended life for many with HIV/AIDS, the treatment protocols are burdensome and expensive. HIV also contributes to poverty, homelessness, and other medical problems.

106. D: It has been estimated that, not only will there be a 50 percent increase in the number of seniors needing substance abuse treatment, but there will also be a 70 percent rate of increase in the treatment needed by these older adults. In part, this may be because baby boomers have had a higher baseline of use throughout their lives than the generations that preceded them. In addition, the baby boomer generation and beyond is more racially and ethnically diverse, with all the unique needs this entails. Barriers to treatment among older adults include: (1) high levels of shame; (2) relatives who either rationalize the problem away or are ashamed to acknowledge it on behalf of their loved one; (3) diagnosis and treatment is more difficult because of collateral mental and physical health problems; (4) transportation is more limited; (5) social networks are dwindling; and (6) financial constraints are tighter.

107. A: When the many barriers to entering treatment are overcome, older adults tend to have substantially better attendance and a significantly lower rate of relapse that are found among younger adults in treatment. Research also indicates that these positive performance measures continue, even if older adults are brought into mixed-age treatment settings. However, the optimum outcomes are dependent upon seniors receiving age-appropriate, individualized treatment services. Seniors often do not envision themselves as abusers—particularly when over-the-counter or prescription drugs are at issue—and they often misunderstand problems arising from alcohol and drug interactions. Consequently, many will need to be reached through health promotion, wellness, social services, and other resources that work with older adults. To this end, program providers need to be involved actively with local aging networks, including home- and community-based short- and long-term care providers. These same external resources can often also assist with specialized cultural, ethnic, and language resources as needed.

108. B: Only mandated reporting information, such as child abuse, can be disclosed without a client's written consent. This includes any information about whether or not a client is receiving treatment or what he or she may be receiving treatment for, even to an employer paying for the treatment. Further, non-court-ordered information cannot be released even to a law enforcement agency or to any other interested party without the client's written consent. A properly informed client is one who is aware of: (1) to whom or what entity the information is being released; (2) the full purpose for the release; (3) the specific information to be released; and (4) when the information release expires. Client confidentiality regarding substance abuse treatment is protected by the Substance Abuse Confidentiality Regulations 42 CFR (Code of Federal Regulations) Part 2 (codified as 42 U.S.C. [United States Code] §290dd-2 and 42 CFR Part 2 (Part 2) and the Health Insurance Portability and Accountability Act (HIPAA, codified as 42 U.S.C. §1320d et seq., 45 CFR Parts 160 and 164).

109. C: The CAGE questionnaire effective and quickly screens for alcohol abuse by asking for a yes or no response to four questions: (1) Have you ever felt the need to cut down on your drinking; (2) do you feel annoyed by people complaining about your drinking; (3) do you ever feel guilty about your drinking; and (4) do you ever drink an eye-opener in the morning to relieve the shakes? Extensive studies reveal that two yes responses will accurately identify 75 percent of the alcoholics who honestly respond to it (and correctly rule out 96 percent of nonalcoholics). The CAGE has been modified to screen for drug abuse by simply replacing the word *drinking* with *drug use* in the initial three questions and then delivering the fourth question: Do you use one drug to change the effects of another drug, or do you ever use drugs first thing in the morning to take the edge off?

110. D: The Michigan Alcoholism Screening Test (MAST) is used in more in-depth interviews as well as in confinement or brief holding scenarios. It is administered to explore a number of important treatment issues: (1) the severity of the alcohol abuse problem; (2) a client's maturity and readiness for treatment; (3) the potential existence of a co-occurring psychiatric disorder; (4) the intervention technique needed to address the presenting problem; (5) the extent of potential support resources (including family, social, educational, and employment resources, along with individual motivation for change); and (6) facilitation of the engagement process leading to treatment. MAST is among the oldest and most accurate alcohol screening instruments and is able to identify dependent drinkers with as much as 98 percent accuracy.

Its two drawbacks are (1) it is longer than many other screening tools, and (2) MAST questions explore drinking over a client's lifetime (not just currently), which makes the test less likely to detect early-stage drinking problems. Several variations of the MAST have been developed, including the brief MAST, the short MAST, and the self-administered MAST.

111. D: The relapse and remitting model of addiction has been successfully applied to a great many other situations, such as unemployment, poor medication compliance, anger management, and so on. Indeed, virtually any situation that tends to return (relapse) can benefit from this model. The relapse and remitting model recognizes that some issues tend to return cyclically over time. Recognizing this can help both the counselor and the client make advance contingency plans to avoid having a brief lapse return to a full relapse in negative circumstances or behaviors. This is particularly important in addiction management as lapses or relapses in any area of life tend to draw clients back into addiction relapses as well. Therefore, careful recognition and following of relapse-prone issues can result in quality advance planning, prompt responses, and minimization or outright prevention of further concurrent addiction relapse problems as well.

112. B: The term *authentically connected referral network* refers to a carefully established set of service providers prepared to meet client needs as they evolve. Key elements to the network are: (1) established communication linkages to facilitate timely sharing of information with client consent; (2) a focus on community-wide outcomes, ensuring that best interests are being met and that community education ensures understandings about substance abuse; (3) a primary focus on meeting client needs through collaboration as opposed to exclusionary rules; (4) consistency and credibility in conduct to ensure both interagency and client confidence and trust. The goal is for all network agencies and providers to recognize their valued and essential roles in the addiction treatment process and for clients to recognize this and respond with similar trust and confidence.

113. C: Although it is important to provide timely and well-coordinated referrals and to encourage client self-determination in this process, it is most important to secure the least-restrictive level of care. In this way, client self-determination is also ensured. To achieve this, clients and case managers must collaborate in selecting among available options. Self-determination is most fully ensured when clients are allowed to take the lead in identifying their needs and in choosing from among resource options that most fully meet their personal goals and lifestyle. Flexibility is important, as is adaptability, to ensure that referral providers and agencies are adequately responsive. Clients should be assessed for their ability to apply for, access, and follow through with selected referrals, with the case manager providing assistance where needed. Informing, educating, and guiding clients through this process can help to ensure an overall least-restrictive level of care.

114. A: When making referrals, it is important to carefully inform clients of your concerns and reasons and then to engage them in ways that do not induce obstruction. The ask-tell-ask technique can assist in this. Further, providing ample information, background, and personal insights into referrals can also assist. To this end, it is important for case managers to be intimately familiar with their referrals, having completed site visits, meeting with provider staff, and in other ways becoming well prepared to put clients' concerns to rest. Finally, all substance abuse communications should be conducted away from clients' families and other staff, and any further sharing should take place only after receiving clients' express permission to that end.

115. D: Referrals are of limited value if they do not contribute measurably to important goals and needed outcomes. These measures of success are evaluated by tracking the results of the referral—ideally, by means of a referral form. The who portion of the form identifies the client and the involved counselor. It may also include demographic information as well as information on the substances the client uses, any legal issues, and family concerns. The what section addresses the issues that generated the need for the referral—substance issues (and symptomatology), work issues, family issues, goals and commitments, and so on. The form's how section should address how the client was engaged and dealt with. In this way, the referrals made for any given client in the how section can be evaluated for interventions provided and outcomes realized.

116. D: The initial contact provides the counselor with the opportunity to gather both positive and negative client history, which should not only be used in treatment plan development and ongoing modification over time but which will be relevant in the aftercare planning process as well. Family members should be drawn into aftercare planning and education early on to ensure ongoing understanding and support. Aftercare planning should also include education regarding health maintenance and prevention against sexually transmitted infections (STIs) – especially human immunodeficiency virus (HIV), tuberculosis, and hepatitis C, among others. Screening for STIs and tuberculosis should be an important part of programming as substance abuse clients may well not recall high-risk behaviors and thus may have encountered diseases of which they are not aware.

117. D: Clients need positive education and skills in substance abuse triggers, patterns of use, and relapse prevention. However, failures in other key areas of clients' lives can also trigger substance abuse relapses. Consequently, holistic treatment planning and interventions are essential to the recovery process. Establishing routine schedules early on can help clients to better organize their lives and sustain abstinence following program completion. Efforts directed toward improvement in the development of life skills can be especially important. Examples include counseling and education in areas such as self-esteem and assertiveness training, communication and anger management skills, relationship training, counseling for co-occurring disorders and personal psychological issues, vocational–educational training and interviewing skills, as well as home maintenance, budgeting and personal hygiene instruction—all are important contributors to clients' abilities to maintain clean and sober lifestyles.

118. A: Trigger events are often crisis stressors or situations (e.g., notice of divorce, job loss, an impending holiday or anniversary, or visiting someone in an old neighborhood where past friends may again invite and encourage using, etc.). Clients are encouraged to anticipate such events and then bookend them—talking about them with a trusted friend (e.g., a twelve-step sponsor, close confidant, trusted friend, etc.) both before and after they occur. In this way, the client can prepare to remain strong and then debrief and decompress emotionally in order to continue strong in his or her abstinence commitments. A counselor can be of further assistance, addressing the client's specific strengths and weaknesses in order to shore up the client's resolve. In this way, the client can be assisted in avoiding a return to past familiar dysfunctional responses.

119. C: The Code of Federal Regulations (CFR) Title 42 Part 2 deals with issues of confidentiality when working with clients coping with drug or alcohol use and abuse. The confidentiality restrictions apply: (1) to records, which may not be disclosed even in administrative, civil, criminal, or legislative proceedings by any governmental authority; (2) to communications, even if the person seeking information already has it, could otherwise obtain it, is an official or law officer, has a subpoena, or otherwise claims the right of information release not permitted in the CFR; and (3) to acknowledgements, such as regarding the presence of a client (unless he or she is in a facility or facility area not dedicated solely to alcohol or drug abuse treatment, and no mention of drug or alcohol treatment is made), whether past, current, or anticipated in the future without the client's written consent. A subpoena will be valid for information release only if a court of competent jurisdiction also explicitly enters an order authorizing information release specific to these regulations.

120. B: The Health Insurance Portability and Accountability Act of 1996 (HIPAA) allows workers and families to retain their health insurance coverage when changing or between jobs. HIPAA also governs the management and release of Protected Health Information (PHI). The act ensures the right to privacy for all adults and minors ages twelve to eighteen. The act requires a signed disclosure before any health care information can be disclosed to any entity, agency, or individual, including parents of minors over the age of twelve. The more stringent guidelines, however, arise from the Code of Federal Regulations (CFR Title 42 Part 2). In 2000, the Department of Health and Human Services (DHHS) issued the Standards for Privacy of Individually Identifiable Health Information. The DHHS Privacy Rule imposed three additional privacy protection steps: (1) consent for information release must comply with 45 CFR §164.508; (2) clients must be given a copy of the signed form; and (3) a copy of each signed form must be kept for six years from its expiration date.

121. D: Every state and all federal regulations allow the limited breach of confidentiality in situations of credible suicidality and threats of serious harm to others. Credible suicidality is a plan for self-harm and the means to carry out the plan. Dangerousness to others typically involves voiced threats regarding a third party and the real intention of harm (possibly including intentional human immunodeficiency virus [HIV] exposures). Tarasoff regulations require a counselor to notify the intended victim or someone reasonably able to notify the intended victim as well as law enforcement. Mandated reporting of child abuse typically involves physical or sexual abuse, though other conditions may apply. Many states have similar laws governing reporting abuse of the elderly or dependent adults. Finally, conditions of grave disability may also require that confidentiality be breached to keep an individual and others safe. Grave disability tends to be defined as compromise from a mental disorder to the extent an individual is not able to pursue basic personal needs (food, clothing, or shelter) or otherwise sustain health and personal safety.

122. A: Just as individual therapy is a far more private, personal, and in-depth therapeutic modality, so is group therapy very different from twelve-step programming. Although both groups are complementary and important, a therapy group focuses on helping individuals to examine, understand, and interpret the intrapsychic and interpersonal influences and conflicts that motivate and perpetuate substance abuse. In contrast to this, twelve-step program practices are centered on drawing upon focuses such as affiliation, peer confrontation and support, and creating a culture of abstinence and the mutual accountability to sustain it. While both modalities can, for example, address denial, the twelve-step process confronts and breaks it down, while group therapy explores what produced it in the first place. Thus, group therapy is far more complex and requires highly specialized skills and experiences to effectively carry it out. Borrowing from twelve-step programming dilutes the group therapy venture and can lead to partial or complete failure of the group therapy process as the profound potential for psychological growth, emotional healing, and self-understanding remain neglected.

123. B: The cognitive-behavioral group model views substance abuse as an issue of dependency and dependency as a learned behavior that can be modified. Modification is accomplished through a variety of interventions such as: (1) identifying the conditioned stimuli that trigger specific addictive behaviors; (2) producing ways to avoid conditioned stimuli; (3) creating contingency management strategies (relapse prevention strategies); and (4) desensitizing stimuli–response patterns. The cognitive-behavioral approach recognizes dependency as arising from the interplay of numerous contributing factors, including: (1) neurobehavioral, (2) biopsychosocial, and (3) genetic and physiological (i.e., the disease model). Cognitive-behavioral therapy groups change perceptions, beliefs, and thinking patterns to alter relapse behaviors and develop social networks to offer support for change.

124. C: There is a myriad of factors to consider in assigning a client to any given group. These include: group availability, client stage in recovery, client preference, gender and culture issues, substance of abuse, and so on. Further, changes in group assignments may be needed episodically as clients progress, relapse, gain motivation, develop new insights needing address, and so on. Diversity issues include age, gender, race, ethnicity, education, language, sexual orientation, religion, and culture, among others. Cultural competence requires a counselor to recognize that: (1) a young Asian male may be unable to express himself openly among older Asians due to issues of respect; (2) many Hispanics or Latinos are adverse to rules and the authority figures that sustain them; (3) women may contend with the need to nurture and invest emotional energy in men; and so on. Adaptations, accommodations, and skillful group leadership will be required to optimize all participants' group opportunities.

125. A: While longer is generally better, the positive effects of treatment duration typically begin to emerge at around three months. In planning treatment, the Institute of Medicine adds: (1) there is no one best treatment approach; (2) inpatient (residential) has not been proven superior to outpatient approaches; (3) outcomes improve if other related life problems are also treated; (4) outcomes are influenced by the treatment process, client–therapist characteristics, aftercare adjustment, and interactions among these variables; (5) many life areas improve with significant reductions in use or total abstinence. Finally, when comparing the management success of chronic ongoing-maintenance medical conditions (asthma, diabetes, and hypertension) with relapse rates for cocaine, nicotine, and opiates, the overall treatment response rates were similar, highlighting the similar compliance and behavioral change requirements involved and human nature in meeting these requirements.

126. A: The three most common recovery stages are described as: early recovery, middle recovery, and late recovery or maintenance. Key features of early recovery include entering treatment, embarking on abstinence, and staying sober. Early recovery, however, is very fragile, and relapse vulnerability remains high. This stage of recovery typically lasts from one month to one year. Key features of middle recovery include: greater confidence in abstinence grows; cravings persist but are recognized and deflected successfully; lifestyle and personality trait changes are progressing; and although relapse vulnerability persists, it is becoming less significant. Middle recovery lasts at least a year but may continue indefinitely (failing to progress or serial relapsing). Key features of late recovery or the maintenance stage are: maintaining abstinence while also improving life in other related areas; addressing psychological or relationship issues that became apparent through abstinence; and continuing all relapse prevention behaviors and skills previously learned.

127. B: Other expressive therapies include writing (stories, poetry, etc.) and music. Expressive group therapy allows clients various ways of expressing themselves via alternative methods and allows greater exploration of their thoughts, bodies, and feelings. Through creative expression, clients can tap into their imaginations to better and more safely examine their bodies, feelings, emotions, and thought processes. Culturally specific groups provide opportunities to explore the role of culture in substance abuse and the strengths and handicaps it may produce during the change process. Relapse prevention groups offer clients the opportunity to focus intensely on developing the skills they need to identify, understand, and manage the situations, people, and thoughts that may trigger a return to substance abuse. Each of these groups can be used concurrently with client participation in other groups, augmenting and enhancing the learning and change processes.

128. C: All groups pass through five phases to accomplish their purposes: forming, storming, norming, performing, and adjourning (last phase added in 1977). Forming involves engaging, exchanging information, and creating bonds. The key characteristics are tentative overtures, polite exchanges, and worries about fitting in. Storming involves dissatisfaction, disagreement, competition, and conflict. Key characteristics are criticizing ideas, interrupting, hostility, and attendance issues. Norming involves forming group structure, establishing roles and relationships, developing cohesion, and creating harmony. Key characteristics are seeking consensus, reaching agreements, creating support, and achieving a sense of we in endeavors. Performing involves task focus, emphasizing productivity, and identifying achievements. Key characteristics are cooperation, problem solving, and decision making. Adjourning involves completing tasks, ending duties, and dropping dependency. Key characteristics are feeling regrets, managing emotions, and disbanding.

129. C: Productive groups not infrequently elicit strong responses. The group experience is enhanced by: (1) self-disclosure that is genuine rather than contrived, honestly reflecting feelings, attitudes, and struggles; (2) authentic behavior that reflects the real self as opposed to the socially presented self, or the front used to avoid criticism and rejection; (3) personal risk taking, usually initiated by a leader, leading to the openness and candor that allows for actual growth and progress; (4) personal privacy, secured by group consensus and commitment to such a degree that self-disclosure, authentic behavior, and risk taking are possible. It should be noted that the key contributions already noted are to be exercised in balance and moderation. All expressions should be self-oriented, revealing oneself rather than pushing through into the private space of others. In this way, negative exchanges among group members can be avoided. Group leaders, while modeling, should be careful not to over-disclose to avoid damaging confidence and trust.

130. B: Families alter normal behaviors in many ways to cope with substance abuse and addiction. Children are likely to assume roles and responsibilities beyond those of their normal maturational development. They may miss out on their childhood, having to cope with insecurities and anxieties that are distorting and deforming of the normal developmental processes. Spouses and intimate others develop compensating behaviors such as denial and cover-up strategies to try and cope socially. Aging parents have to skip the normal launching phase that most young adults prepare for and achieve. Friends, neighbors, and coworkers have to adjust to their unreliability. Moreover, abusers often abandon or estrange themselves from their families, choosing reinforcing associations with other users in order to cope with their increasing antisocial and isolating needs. Children, in particular, are likely to telescope these issues intergenerationally as they grow up to become overprotective, overly controlling, dependent, or otherwise unbalanced in their own marriages (which may then fail) and in their parenting practices (which distort the experiences of the next generation, etc.).

131. C: Approximately 25% of all human immunodeficiency virus (HIV) cases are among adolescent and adult females in the United States. Although HIV continues to predominantly affect men who are sexually active with other men (homosexual or bisexual gay males), women are particularly susceptible to contracting the HIV virus. Due to many factors, African American and Hispanic or Latina women account for more than four-fifths of all HIV cases among women. At highest risk of new infection, however, are gay people who abuse substances as this group is also most likely to engage in risky sexual behavior. Other factors that contribute to issues of risk are: substance abuse, homelessness and poverty, psychiatric disorders, living in chaotic and high-crime areas, and so on. The incidence of substance abuse among those with HIV is higher than the national average, in part, no doubt, to issues of stress and depression that accompany the diagnosis. Although newer treatment options improve the overall outcome somewhat, obtaining treatment and maintaining the complex treatment regimen required is far more difficult among those who abuse alcohol and other substances.

132. C: On all measures of alcohol and drug use and abuse, the incidence of occurrence is higher. The lesbian, gay, bisexual, and transgender (LGBT) community has a greater likelihood of alcohol and drug use generally, are more likely to abuse these substances, are less likely to maintain abstinence, and continue alcohol use longer into their later years. Research reveals that as high as 30 percent of the lesbian community may have a drinking problem. In addition, LGBT substance abusers tend to use more frequently and more kinds of drugs. In particular, judgment-altering drugs are also more common (e.g., amyl nitrite, gamma hydroxybutyrate, ketamine, and ecstasy). The more frequent use of judge-altering drugs such as those at raves and parties appears to be correlated with the higher rates of human immunodeficiency virus (HIV) infection due to a greater frequency of higher-risk sexual behaviors. Unquestionably, this community would benefit from greater education, services, and specially oriented groups and services.

133. A: Given their disabilities, those who are cognitive or physically disabled are unable to find work and yet also spend a larger share of their income to meet the needs of their disabilities. Consequently, poverty, depression, unmedicated pain, functional limits, and vocational difficulties leave this group particularly vulnerable to drug and alcohol abuse. Further, because of these same cognitive or functional disabilities, coupled with limitations in networks and resources, members of this group are not only more likely to develop a substance abuse problem but less likely to receive treatment for the problems they do develop. In particular, learning disabilities are common among this population, and these learning obstacles also make what treatment they do receive less effective. In consequence, programs more carefully tailored to the needs of this population are very much needed.

134. A: Older adults are particularly receptive to treatment for drug and alcohol abuse. However, they are less likely to be identified as having a problem compared with the general population. The reasons for this include: (1) they are more likely to feel shame over the problem; (2) they are more likely to be covert about any substance abuse problems; (3) they are less likely to recognize they have a problem as much of the abuse may involve prescription medications, which they tend to justify; (4) they are unaware of interaction problems between alcohol and prescription drugs; (5) they often have physical conditions that may obscure their substance abuse, making it difficult to diagnose. Because of these factors, abuse among the elderly may more likely be spotted via screenings at wellness centers than by drug abuse outreach programs. Finally, this population has special needs, and age-appropriate treatment is essential for optimal outcomes.

135. C: Substance abuse issues may develop at any time throughout the life course, especially during times of stress, divorce, family discord, unemployment, pain-inducing injury, depression, and other particularly vulnerable periods. Overall, however, the period of greatest risk is adolescence. This group is particularly vulnerable for numerous reasons, including: (1) the developing brain (during childhood and adolescence) is more susceptible to the changes induced by addiction; (2) the likelihood of exposure to substances of abuse increases at this time; (3) immaturity makes it more difficult to cope with peer pressure; (4) underdeveloped judgment (typically generating a sense of invulnerability) makes the desire for risk taking greater; (5) transitional stressors moving toward adulthood increase the need for alternative coping options, particularly those with little developmental demands; (6) the social demands of school and relationships become more acute; (7) hormonal and other developmental changes induce further instability. Programs sensitive to these needs are greatly needed in the substance abuse treatment field.

136. D: A great many science-informed, effective prevention programs have been designed to target youth of varying ages in a variety of settings. There are three types of youth substance abuse prevention programs: (1) universal programs—designed to address both risk and protective factors in the general community or in school settings; (2) selective programs—oriented to engage youth that possess specifically identified risk factors that increase their likelihood of developing a substance abuse disorder; and (3) indicated programs—designed to address issues relevant to youth who have already allowed substance abuse into their lives. When programs such as these are properly applied to age-appropriate target audiences, research reveals that abuse of drugs, alcohol, and tobacco are all reduced. Central to all these programs is education regarding the harms caused by substance abuse as such education has proven to reduce experimentation and lower the rates of continued substance abuse in youth.

137. B: Clients are not a party to documentation in records except in the rarest of circumstances. Rather, the need for accurate documentation is essential in determining a proper treatment plan and ensuring that the plan evolves appropriately as the client makes continued progress. Further, funding agencies require documentation to ensure that funds entrusted to the program are being utilized as agreed upon in the funding process. Overall, essential documentation competencies include: (1) recording of intake and screening; (2) client assessment; treatment plan formulation and goals; (3) clinical reports; (4) clinician progress notes; (5) a comprehensive discharge summary; and (6) any other client-related information or data necessary to ensure appropriate compliance, understanding, and treatment selection (e.g., consent forms, etc.). Client records should be safely maintained and stored in accordance with existing city, county, state, and federal regulations.

138. A: It is very important to document all referrals made along with related outcomes. In this way, the full range of services a client is receiving and has received is known, and the effectiveness of any referral services can also be followed and measured over time. However, referrals are not part of the intake and evaluation process. Essential intake assessment information includes: (1) psychoactive substance abuse history and patterns of use; (2) psychological health and psychiatric treatment history; (3) current physiological health, nutrition, and medical history; (4) medications history and current medications; (5) basic demographic and social information; (6) legal history (arrests, sentences, probation or parole status, etc.); (7) educational history; (8) recreational activity history; (9) religious or spiritual history and current beliefs; (10) sexual orientation; (11)

high-risk sexual and substance use practices, if any; and (12) family history and current support network.

139. C: Relevant changes might arise if a client tests positive for an addictive substance, if mandatory meetings are missed, if an ancillary support program terminates services, or where substantial progress is noted. While formats may vary, the flow of information in a treatment or recovery plan remains consistent: (1) alcohol or drug-related problems are listed, including social, vocational, family, and medical problems; (2) current short- and long-term objectives; (3) action plans that will meet short-term goals; (4) client progress measures toward identified goals; and (5) updates to the discharge summary or continuing care plan as ongoing changes warrant. In this way, the treatment and recovery plan remains actively applicable, and client progress can be carefully monitored and followed.

140. D: Properly written progress notes chart the trajectory of the client's progress toward the goals, objectives, and action steps that make up the treatment plan. Progress notes are used to explain and inform any changes to the treatment plan in the context of what is actually happening in the client's daily lived experiences, behaviors, and level of functioning. In order to maintain a current and effective treatment plan, progress notes must be recorded within fourteen days or less of counseling sessions and fully reviewed at the time of a treatment plan update. These updates occur at regularly scheduled intervals or whenever it becomes apparent that changes in client functioning, behavior, motivation, or intent warrant the update. In this way, the treatment plan remains informative, effective, and transformational.

141. A: No information should be obliterated in a client record. It is only appropriate to line it out with a single line and indicate that the information was entered in error, when, and by whom. Generally, black ink should be used, every page should have a header with the client's name, and all notes should be concluded with the author's signature and any relevant acronym indicating a relevant degree, certification, or licensure. All notes should address interventions and client responses along with references to any related goals or objectives. No other clients should be named in another client's record, limiting references to others by the first name or initials only, if necessary, or by relationship status if adequately clear. Blank areas on a page should be avoided. If a blank space is left, it should be lined through with one or more diagonal lines. Charts should never leave a facility except for purposes of audit.

142. C: Whether the client's treatment includes group or individual session counseling, most states require an updating entry at least weekly. Entries should include session dates and attendance status as well as client progress in terms of recovery phase and movement toward (or away from) recovery or treatment goals and objectives. Entries should clearly indicate whether the progress (or lack of progress) leaves the client on or off track in regards to achieving necessary progress, especially if an associated increase in relapse risk has been identified. Issues of client responsiveness to program staff, involved family, referral services, as well as attendance compliance should be noted in an ongoing fashion. Finally, planned or expected interventions and recommendations should also be included in the weekly update or summary entry.

143. B: A comprehensive discharge summary is always produced, regardless of how long or short the client's involvement was in the treatment program. Specifically required content includes: (1) whether the program was or was not completed successfully; (2) the reasons or rationale that resulted in client discharge; (3) whether the discharge was voluntary or involuntary; (4) any transfer or referrals involved in the discharge, with specific information about each, including transfer or referral rationale; (5) summary information on treatments offered and recovery level achieved; (6) the client's status in abstinence or continued substance use; (7) educational or vocational accomplishments; (8) legal status at the point of discharge; (9) relevant continuing medical issues, if any; and (10) any involved supports or services that are expected to be continued beyond discharge.

144. D: In general, the language in 42 CFR Part 2 prevents all information releases (as well as client-identifying information), even to other uninvolved staff. Key exceptions do, however, exist: (1) written information releases—if properly completed—oral consent, however, is not permitted; (2) emergency medical situations—limited essential information may be given to treating medical personnel but not to law enforcement directly; (3) other agencies working with a client—if a Qualified Service Organization Agreement (QSOA) that guarantees confidentiality at the same level has been signed; (4) mandated reports—notifying authorities of child abuse, and (sometimes) dependent adult and elder abuse, releasing only limited essential information; (5) qualified researchers under limited conditions; (6) crime on site or against staff—limited release to law enforcement; and (7) court order or subpoena, search warrant, or arrest warrant—only if it also meets 42 CFR Part 2 criteria. Language in 42 CFR Part 2 also applies to all staff and volunteers as well as past, current, and even potential (applicant) clients, living or deceased.

145. D: The Code of Federal Regulations, Part 2, Subpart E, requires that information, even about the mere presence of a client in treatment, is not to be released under any circumstances unless a qualified court hearing has first been held wherein the issue of confidentiality and client needs have first been addressed. Following this, a special authorizing order must be issued. At a hearing, the court must determine: (1) if the alleged crime is sufficiently serious to warrant breaching confidentiality in this sensitive area (e.g., homicide, rape, assault with a deadly weapon, etc.); (2) if the records disclosure will be of sufficient value in the investigation; (3) if other reasonably effective options exist; (4) if the potential for damage to the client, to the client–provider relationship, and to the program's ability to continue providing services outweighs the release of this very sensitive information; and (5) if the applicant is acting in a true law enforcement function and if adequate counsel has been obtained by the records holder or agency.

146. C: Substance abuse clients, especially those with a history of abuse themselves, can struggle with impulse control and emotions, especially anger. Acting out anger cannot be tolerated. Usually, however, there are signs of agitation, elevation, and anger well before physical acting out occurs. At this earlier juncture, it can be helpful for the counselor to validate their affect without validating any given verbal expression ("I can see this is something difficult for you . . ." or "This brings up a lot of emotion for you, doesn't it?"). In this way, the counselor moves to constructive address of the client's emotions, defusing the need to act out physically. Prevention is particularly valuable—ground rules for conduct in group, with staff and on site, should be provided at the point of intake. Language, breach of confidentiality, threats, and physical aggression cannot be tolerated. Law enforcement may need to be called if safety becomes an issue. Clients should know in advance that serious threats are taken seriously and will be reported.

147. B: Many substance-abusing clients suffer from low self-esteem, poor self-control, deficient boundaries, and high impulsivity. Where this behavior is the result of poor emotional control, various interventions may help. Where the problem arises from underlying pathology (e.g., posttraumatic stress disorder [PTSD], bipolar disorder, psychosis, intoxication, etc.), rapid de-escalation and backup support may be immediately necessary. Where the behavior is simply developmental immaturity, grounding techniques are often beneficial. In anchoring, the counselor leads the client to relax, close his or her eyes, and focus on breathing and the immediate environment (the chair, the room, the quiet, etc.). Then, the counselor has the client recognize that, in spite of worries about the past or future, the immediate present is safe. The counselor must support this by avoiding sudden movements, pressured speech, and so on, so as to avoid any

M⊘metrix

hypervigilant response from the client. In mirroring, the counselor has the client synchronize his or her breathing with the counselor's, leading to a calm rate (counselors avoid this technique if transference intimacy has been an issue). In timeout, the counselor allows the client to take a break from the topic, leaving the room if necessary, to relax before continuing.

148. A: Many survivors of significant abuse tend to put themselves in further high-risk situations. Their countertransference issues with the counselor may draw the counselor into the role of rescuer as they seek the safety, nurturance, and security they deeply desire. If the counselor is not fully self-aware, he or she can be pulled into this dynamic in seeking to defend and support the client. In doing so, however, the client moves into dependency and fails to learn how to identify and set appropriate boundaries in his or her own life. Over time, the concerned counselor may over treat, lend funds, arrange child care, and otherwise inappropriately respond. The counselor may also attempt to intervene with others on the client's behalf and find him- or herself polarized from a client that is now angry with the counselor for intruding into important family or other relationships. While rescuing may temporarily relieve the counselor's concerns and frustrations, it will never provide long-term resolution of the problems.

149. C: Counselors must recognize that they are also entitled to limits. While working with difficult clients is a part of the job, it does not require working in situations that are personally deeply disturbing or troubling. It can also lead to substandard service for the client, who is entitled to receive counseling from a professional who is not compromised by his or her past history. In situations such as this, it may be helpful to seek supervisory consultation to better determine what is occurring and the degree of the associated problem. The client should be notified in advance of the need (but not the direct reason) for a transfer to avoid generating issues of rejection or abandonment. He or she should be informed that another clinician better suited to meeting his or her needs is available. Any subsequent issues about the transfer should also be addressed in the new therapeutic relationship.

150. D: While an agency must continue to receiving funding, provide employment, and maintain a consistent reputation in order to continue offering services, its most important purpose and function is to break the cycle of abuse and relieve the individual, involved families, and society as a whole from the suffering involved. To accomplish this, staff must receive appropriate support. This involves proper supervision and training, avoiding over-scheduling caseloads, allowing time for colleague consultations and support, facilitating quality outside support and consultation as needed, providing policies and procedures that ensure a safe, effective, and positive work environment, and so on. In this way, staff can be supported, quality services will be provided, agency longevity will be maintained, and turnover and burnout will be kept to a minimum. Administrators must recognize that counselors can only be expected to perform optimally if agency leadership provides adequate support.

Practice Test #2

1. What are withdrawal symptoms, characterized by severe flu-like symptoms (nausea, vomiting, runny nose, watery eyes, chills, abdominal cramps, anorexia, weakness, tremors, sweating, etc.), MOST characteristic?
   a. Opioid withdrawal
   b. Hallucinogenic withdrawal
   c. Barbiturate withdrawal
   d. Benzodiazepine withdrawal

2. Genetic factors make up roughly what proportion of the risk for addiction?
   a. Less than one-tenth
   b. One-quarter
   c. One-half
   d. Three-quarters

3. What is the adolescent tendency to impulsivity and risk taking due to primarily?
   a. Poor parenting
   b. Prior abuse
   c. Neurological immaturity
   d. Influences of puberty

4. What are depressant drugs (e.g., alcohol, opiates, barbiturates, and benzodiazepines) typically used to cope with?
   a. Excitement
   b. Fatigue
   c. Stress
   d. Boredom

5. Past which point is benzodiazepine treatment of anxiety NOT effective?
   a. Six weeks
   b. Four months
   c. One year
   d. Eighteen months

6. At low doses, what does alcohol act as physiologically?
   a. Stimulant
   b. Psychedelic
   c. Depressant
   d. Hallucinogenic

7. Among the following, what is the MOST harmful drug a mother can abuse during pregnancy?
   a. Heroin
   b. Lysergic Acid (LSD)
   c. Alcohol
   d. Methamphetamine

58

8. Theorists posit that stimulant abuse often occurs to compensate for deficiencies in all of the following neurotransmitters EXCEPT

    a. norepinephrine.
    b. acetylcholine.
    c. serotonin.
    d. dopamine.

9. What is the euphoria experienced when under the influence of cocaine caused by?

    a. A cascade-effect of endorphins
    b. A sudden release of adrenalin
    c. Increased basal metabolic rate
    d. A buildup of neurotransmitters

10. What kind of drug does the term *nootropic* refer to?

    a. Memory enhancing
    b. Mood stabilizing
    c. Hallucinogenic
    d. Psychedelic

nootropic = memory

11. Which of the following is NOT a stage in the development of alcoholism?

    a. Dependent drinking
    b. Morning drinking
    c. Social drinking
    d. Heavy drinking

12. In the lifecycle of heroin addiction, what is the stage known as disjunction characterized by?

    a. Entrance into the addiction subculture
    b. Episodic binge use of heroin in social settings
    c. Serial treatment, abstinence and relapses
    d. Crime, arrests, imprisonment, and serial treatment

disjunction   disfunction

13. Which of the following is NOT a typical stage in the development of cocaine addiction?

    a. Compulsive use
    b. Experimental use
    c. Isolated use
    d. Dysfunctional use

14. Social control theorists suggest that deviance results from which TWO of the following?

    a. Poor socioeconomic conditions
    b. Weak societal ties with the individual
    c. Weak familial ties with the individual
    d. Confining societal expectations

15. Withdrawal symptoms from anabolic steroids most closely resemble those of which drug?

    a. Marijuana
    b. Heroin
    c. Amphetamines
    d. Cocaine

16. Which is the MOST correct statement regarding individuals voluntarily entering treatment for substance?

    a. They are committed to change.
    b. They are fully ready to change.
    c. They are at varying stages of change readiness.
    d. They are primarily in need of encouragement.

17. What is ambivalence about substance abuse treatment symptomatic?

    a. Resistance
    b. Denial
    c. Uncertainty
    d. Confrontation

18. What is the primary goal of screening a client with a known substance abuse disorder?

    a. Get rid of those clients with serious problems
    b. Determine a best initial treatment course
    c. Discover any dual diagnoses
    d. Evaluate the likely length of treatment needed

19. In screening clients, what does a cutoff score refer to?

    a. A criteria-based score beyond which a client must be turned away
    b. The threshold above which a more thorough assessment is indicated
    c. A score that is incomplete, having been cut off prematurely
    d. The final score that supersedes any other screening score obtained

20. What is the suicide risk for individuals treated for alcohol use disorder?

    a. About the same as for the general population
    b. Two times as high as among the general population
    c. Five times as high as among the general population
    d. Ten times as high as among the general population

21. Which one of the following MOST properly defines screening and assessment?

    a. Screening evaluates a problem; assessment diagnoses it.
    b. Screening identifies a problem; assessment treats it
    c. Screening looks for a problem; assessment defines it.
    d. Screening reveals a problem; assessment resolves it.

22. When does assessment of a client with co-occurring disorders occur?

    a. Following an initial screening
    b. During the process of intake
    c. Upon confirmation of diagnosis
    d. Regularly over time

23. Which is the gold standard assessment tool for co-occurring disorders?

a. The Addiction Severity Index (ASI)
b. The Minnesota Multiphasic Personality Inventory (MMPI)
c. The Mental Status Exam (MSE)
d. None of the above

24. During assessment, what does the term *collateral contacts* refer to?

a. Contacts with family
b. Contacts with friends
c. Contacts with treatment providers
d. All of the above

25. Which of the following is NOT included in basic intake information?

a. Feelings about institutional treatment (treatment readiness, etc.)
b. Background (family, legal, employment, etc.)
c. Substance use (first use, current drugs, treatment, etc.)
d. Mental health (diagnoses, hospitalizations, treatment, etc.)

26. Which of the following instruments is used to screen for substance abuse in individuals who frequently distort or misrepresent the truth?

a. MAST
b. SASSI
c. SBIRT
d. ASI

27. Which of the following is NOT a key informational outcome of screening and assessment?

a. Measures of client treatment compliance
b. Essential consents and authorizations
c. Substance abuse disorder severity
d. Client strengths and available supports

28. Which of the following is NOT a key goal and purposes of assessment?

a. Identifying the optimum form of intervention for the presenting problem
b. Identifying the resources available for successful problem resolution
c. Whether or not a substance or alcohol problem exists
d. Extent and severity of the substance or alcohol abuse problem

29. What must treatment planning discussions with clients be like?

a. Appropriate to client age and developmental level
b. Sensitive to issues of race, ethnicity, and culture
c. Free of technical jargon and obscure acronyms
d. All of the above

30. Why should data and findings from the assessment be presented to the client and his or her significant others?

a. The client is paying for the service.
b. Staff need to justify what they are doing.
c. Client understanding affects treatment.
d. Client problems need to be aired openly.

61

31. What does the treatment term matching refer to?

    a. Selecting resources by client needs and preferences
    b. Pairing clients into supportive treatment dyads
    c. Sequencing treatment modalities for maximum benefit
    d. Reciprocal communication to ensure client support

32. Which of the following does NOT address patient placement criteria (PPC)?

    a. Substance abuse admission criteria
    b. Continuing stay criteria
    c. Outcome measurement criteria
    d. Discharge or transfer criteria

33. What is a client's readiness for treatment strongly associated?

    a. Duration of time abusing a drug of choice
    b. The perception of needing help in change
    c. Number of deteriorative health changes encountered
    d. Increased cost of the primary drug of choice

34. What does the term *treatment sequencing* refer to?

    a. The order of medications administration
    b. Movement through the levels of care
    c. Using credentialed staff before non-credentialed staff
    d. Prioritizing client needs in the treatment process

35. How is Maslow's Hierarchy of Needs BEST described?

    a. A fundamental ranking of essential needs
    b. The way a client selects a drug of choice
    c. A scale for determining treatment readiness
    d. A model of the processes involved in change

36. Which of the following levels was NOT proposed by Abraham Maslow in his Hierarchy of Needs?

    a. Basic needs
    b. Safety needs
    c. Recreational needs
    d. Esteem needs

37. Information gathering and assessment can be biased if a clinician

    a. uses very general questions.
    b. uses open-ended leading questions.
    c. uses professional jargon.
    d. uses all of the above.

38. What does the Biopsychosocial Model suggest that problems have?

    a. Both mental and physical aspects and origins
    b. An underlying medical or physical etiology
    c. Sociocultural and biological causative factors
    d. Numerous causal factors that are interconnected

39. What is the Chemical Use, Abuse, and Dependence (CUAD) Scale BEST known for?

   a. Its use in substance abuse screening and assessment
   b. Its utility in assessing substance abuse in mentally ill clients
   c. Its ability to producing a *Diagnostic and Statistical Manual of Mental Disorders* (DSM) diagnosis of substance abuse disorder
   d. Its brevity and the minimal administration training required

CUAD = MAD

40. What is the Symptom Checklist-90-R (SCL-90-R) used for?

   a. An in-depth assessment of physiological health
   b. An in-depth assessment of psychological health
   c. Tracking client progress or treatment outcomes
   d. Both B and C

41. What is the COPES scale used for?

   a. Helping clients learn how to cope with transitions
   b. Exploring client readiness for treatment
   c. Assessing client support systems and resources
   d. Assessing community-based treatment programs

COPES = Community

42. What does the TSR assessment instrument measure?

   a. Therapeutic intensity and problem severity
   b. Solution-oriented therapeutic resistance
   c. Nature and intensity of treatment services
   d. Topic-specific remedial outcomes

43. What does the BIRP progress note acronym stand for?

   a. Behavior, Interview, Reaction, Purpose
   b. Behavior, Integrate, Review, Propose
   c. Behavior, Intervention, Response, Plan
   d. Behavior, Intervene, Revise, Program

44. What does the CHEAP progress note acronym stand for?

   a. Chief complaint, History, Evaluation, Action, and Plan
   b. Chief complaint, History, Exam, Assessment, and Plan
   c. Chief complaint, History, Evidence, Attention, and Plan
   d. Chief complaint, History, Evaluation, Axes, and Plan

45. The mnemonic SIGECAPS evaluates which psychological state?

   a. Depression
   b. Anxiety
   c. Paranoia
   d. Mania

Sigecaps = CrCaps

46. What do the acronyms CART and CHART both refer to?

   a. Treatment interventions
   b. Diagnostic assessments
   c. Progress note formats
   d. Assessments for symptoms

 Notes.

47. What does the term *client matching* refer to?

a. Tailoring resources and services to the client needs
b. Obtaining a sponsor for mutual-help program enrollment
c. Finding a treatment buddy during a residential stay
d. Picking the proper level of service intensity

48. The statement "Clients must always hit bottom to be ready for treatment" is

a. absolutely true.
b. partly true.
c. absolutely false.
d. partly false.

49. How is client motivation for treatment BEST maintained?

a. Declarations of serious consequences
b. Fear of failure and the results that follow
c. Reminders of what brought them to treatment
d. Devil's advocate statements that they'll never make it

50. What does client resistance to treatment MOST likely indicate?

a. The client is being pressured to change too quickly.
b. The client simply doesn't care to overcome the problem.
c. The client has been coerced into treatment.
d. The client is embarrassed about past relapses.

51. What is the factor that contributes MOST meaningfully to client treatment retention?

a. Program location and transportation support
b. The therapeutic alliance
c. Family insistence on treatment
d. Court orders for treatment

52. Which of the following treatment episodes is associated with better outcomes?

a. Longer episodes are superior to shorter episodes.
b. Shorter episodes are superior to longer episodes.
c. The length of the treatment episode is not relevant.
d. Completion of any length episode is most important.

53. What should the position of treatment programs toward twelve-step programs be?

a. Clients should not be discouraged from twelve-step programs.
b. Clients should be encouraged to participate in twelve-step programs.
c. Twelve-step programs are a helpful social tool but have no other impact.
d. Twelve-step programs are an integral part of overall client success.

54. Which statement BEST reflects the nature of mutual-help groups such as twelve-step programs?

a. These programs vary greatly and should be carefully chosen.
b. These programs are generally very much the same.
c. These programs are only for substance abusers.
d. These programs are primarily religious in nature and orientation.

64

55. How is the proper role for mental health medications in individuals with co-occurring disorders BEST described?

a. There is no place for mental health medications in the treatment of clients with a substance abuse problem.
b. Clients with a substance abuse disorder and a co-occurring mental health disorder can benefit from medications.
c. Clients with a substance abuse disorder and a co-occurring mental health disorder can take mental health medications without any concern.
d. Clients with a substance abuse disorder and a co-occurring mental health disorder will always benefit from long-term pharmacotherapy.

56. What is the purpose of open-ended heterogeneous groups?

a. To allow flexibility in new member assignments
b. To keep difficult clients away from each other
c. To put clients together with similar issues
d. To meet the needs of clients with special problems

57. What is the purpose of client-specific groups?

a. To meet unique client needs
b. To facilitate the counseling process
c. Both A and B
d. Neither A or B

58. Clients that should never be assigned to the same group include all of the following EXCEPT

a. abuse perpetrators and victims.
b. neighbors and relatives.
c. schizophrenia and antisocial disordered.
d. opioid and amphetamine abusers. Can be in same group

59. During the initial treatment phase, how many therapeutic contact hours per week does the American Society of Addiction Medicine (ASAM) require for intensive outpatient treatment (IOT) participants?

a. Three hours
b. Five hours
c. Seven hours
d. Nine hours

60. Optimal group size in a typical treatment group involves how many members?

a. Eight to fifteen members
b. Six to Twelve members
c. Five to ten members
d. Four to eight members   8-15

61. Which of the following medications is NOT commonly used in the treatment of alcohol abuse?

    a. Disulfiram
    b. Buprenorphine
    c. Acamprosate
    d. Naltrexone

62. Which of the following medications is NOT commonly used in the treatment of opioid abuse?

    a. Luminal
    b. Methadone
    c. Buprenorphine
    d. Levo-alpha acetyl methadol

Luminal = barbiturate

63. The American Society of Addiction Medicine (ASAM) recommends patients with co-occurring disorders be placed in a specialty addiction and mental health treatment program at which level of mental illness severity?

    a. No co-occurring disorder
    b. Mild to low co-occurring severity
    c. Moderate co-occurring severity
    d. High co-occurring severity

64. What are the most common biological samples used for treatment program drug testing?

    a. Hair and sweat
    b. Blood and saliva
    c. Urine and breath
    d. None of the above

65. Which one of the following is not an established twelve-step program?

    a. Narcotics Anonymous
    b. Cocaine Anonymous
    c. Hallucinogens Anonymous
    d. Alcoholics Anonymous

66. What is the ADS scale used to measure?

    a. Alcohol dependence
    b. Anomalous drug use
    c. Readiness for treatment
    d. Substance use minimization

Alcohol dependence scale

67. What is the CIDI instrument is used to measure?

    a. Psychiatric disorders
    b. Substance use disorders
    c. Both A and B
    d. Neither A nor B

68. Which of the following is NOT measured by the DIS schedule?

a. Substance use disorders

b. Alcohol use disorders

c. Psychiatric disorders

d. Physical health disorders

69. For which of the following setting is the MINI designed?

a. Clinical trials

b. Treatment outcome assessments

c. Epidemiological studies

d. All of the above

70. Psychiatric Research Interview for Substance and Mental Disorders (PRISM) evaluates for which of the following distinct personality disorders?

a. Paranoid and obsessive-compulsive

b. Antisocial and borderline

c. Histrionic and narcissistic

d. Avoidant and dependent

71. How is the term _genogram_ BEST defined?

a. A diagram of family relationships

b. A genetic predisposition to addiction

c. A pictogram of intergenerational addiction

d. A phenotype predisposing alcoholism

72. How is the CRAFT program or approach BEST described?

a. A consensus approach to motivating a client into treatment

b. A confrontational approach to motivating a client into treatment

c. A community or family approach to motivating a client into treatment

d. A consciousness-raising approach to motivating a client into treatment

73. What are family education groups primarily designed to do?

a. Provide family and couples therapy

b. Resolve situations of domestic abuse

c. Teach anger management and coping

d. Educate families about addiction

74. What is the difference between a lapse and relapse?

a. Insignificant, as they are interchangeable terms

b. A single use episode versus prolonged use

c. Using a drug of choice versus polydrug use

d. Prolonged drug use versus a single episode.

75. What is the influence of a famous client in group MOST likely to be?

a. Positive, increasing group morale

b. Neutral, becoming just another group member

c. Negative, disrupting group dynamics

d. Uncertain, depending upon the personality

67

76. A potential client enters a program for treatment and a counselor recognizes him from a Little League team in which their sons are both still active. What is the BEST response by the counselor?

    a. Pretend to have not seen the acquaintance, and never speak of it to them.
    b. Speak with the client privately, and offer assurances of confidentiality.
    c. Seek to be assigned as the client's counselor to ease tension and show support.
    d. Refer the client to another treatment program.

77. What is the AASE scale used to determine or evaluate?

    a. Alcohol abstinence commitment in high-relapse situations
    b. Activities and actions used to ensure substance abstinence
    c. Assessment of associations for substance experimentation
    d. Alcohol associations and effects in varying intoxicated states

78. What is the purpose of the AEQ instrument?

    a. To evaluate the quality and efficacy of abstinence
    b. To assesses expected positive and negative effects of alcohol
    c. To assess the qualities of a client's social support network
    d. To question the effects of abstinence education on treatment acceptance

79. What is the ASRPT instrument used for?

    a. To determine whether posttraumatic stress is a component in drinking
    b. To gauge the effectiveness of relaxation therapy in maintaining abstinence
    c. To evaluate stress response features in alcohol relapse situations
    d. To role-play client responses to situations that pose a threat of relapse

80. What is the SCQ designed to do?

    a. Reveal a client's situational confidence in high-risk drinking situations
    b. Evaluate a client's susceptibility to emotional pressures to drink
    c. Assess a client's self-control quotient when experiencing key triggers
    d. Evaluate the qualities driving the context of a client's substance use

81. Cognitive-behavioral therapy (CBT) does NOT address which of the following?

    a. Replacing substance abuse coping with more effective coping skills
    b. Identifying personal cues or triggers that lead to substance abuse
    c. Learning new problem-solving skills and strategies to counteract substance abuse urges
    d. The role of a higher power in achieving and maintaining abstinence

82. Which of the following is NOT a strength of cognitive-behavioral therapy (CBT)?

    a. It is suitable for clients from diverse cultures and other unique backgrounds.
    b. CBT was developed as an effective group counseling approach.
    c. It provides an understanding of relapse triggers and relapse situations.
    d. It accommodates clients with widely varying histories of alcohol and drug use.

83. Which of the following statements is true regarding cognitive-behavioral therapy (CBT)?

    a. It is about as effective as minimal or no therapy at all.
    b. It is inferior to motivational enhancement therapy (MET).
    c. It is superior to contingency management approaches.
    d. It is less effective than twelve-step facilitation for reducing alcohol use.

84. In motivational interviewing (MI), what is the role of the counselor?

a. An expert, providing unilateral direction and guidance
b. A subordinate, primarily listening and reflecting
c. A coach or consultant, asking key questions for learning
d. An authority figure, creating a professional treatment plan

85. How is motivational enhancement therapy (MET) different from motivational interviewing (MI)?

a. MET incorporates structured assessments and follow-up sessions.
b. MET is more unstructured and free-flowing as compared with MI.
c. MET is entirely reflective and non-determinative as compared with MI.
d. MET requires considerable confrontation and counselor assertiveness.

86. How many treatment weeks are involved in the current Matrix Model program?

a. Twelve weeks
b. Sixteen weeks
c. Twenty-four weeks
d. Thirty-two weeks

87. Which of the following is NOT a group in the Matrix Model of treatment?

a. Early recovery skills groups
b. Relapse prevention groups
c. Family education groups
d. Stress management groups

88. What have efficacy studies of the Matrix Model of treatment found?

a. The model is no more effective than other treatment programs.
b. The model is neutral in outcome efficacy.
c. The model is marginally positive in terms of efficacy.
d. The model is significantly positive in measures of efficacy.

89. Of the following, what are the TWO most significant drawbacks to the Matrix Model?

a. Cognitively impaired clients may have difficulty with some materials, and some clients may be adverse to the highly structured content and scheduling.
b. Significant staff training and ongoing supervision is required, and the intense structure and scheduling may interfere with fully addressing other important nondrug issues.
c. Monitoring progress in twelve-step programs can be difficult, and failing to schedule in leisure activities can lead to noncompliance with the schedule.
d. Many clients may struggle with creating and maintaining an hour-by-hour schedule, and family or others may seek to impose a schedule not desired by the client.

90. What theory is community reinforcement (CR) and contingency management (CM) based upon?

a. Social learning theory
b. Operant conditioning theory
c. Family systems theory
d. Biological-genetic theory

91. Osher and Kofoed developed a staged approach to the treatment of co-occurring disorders that incorporates how many stages?

    a. Two stages
    b. Four stages
    c. Six stages
    d. Eight stages

92. Why do clients with co-occurring psychiatric disorders respond poorly to confrontational counseling approaches?

    a. They can't comprehend what is being asked of them.
    b. They are not properly medicated psychiatrically.
    c. They are passive-aggressive and deliberately obstruct.
    d. They decompensate in stressful interpersonal situations.

93. How is the use of group therapy with co-occurring disorders clients BEST described?

    a. Controversial and complicated
    b. Contraindicated and counterproductive
    c. Of uncertain efficacy in this population
    d. Widely accepted and effective

94. The term *double trouble*, in reference to mutual-help groups, refers to what?

    a. Groups for clients with both psychiatric and substance abuse issues
    b. Groups for clients with both legal and substance abuse issues
    c. Groups for clients with polysubstance abuse concerns
    d. Groups for clients with a personality disorder and substance abuse

95. Why are medication management groups created primarily?

    a. To administer medications to noncompliant clients
    b. To allow clients to participate in medication research trials
    c. To transition clients from one medication to another
    d. To offer education and address compliance concerns

96. Among the following mental health disorders, which one is the MOST influenced by culture?

    a. Schizophrenia
    b. Bipolar disorder
    c. Panic disorder
    d. Depression

97. For the counselor, in which of the following is the influence of culture is MOST likely to be apparent?

    a. Symptom presentation
    b. Screening responses
    c. Mental status examination
    d. Substances used

98. What cultural group is least susceptible to suicide?

    a. Rates are lowest for Hispanic men.
    b. Rates are lowest for African American women.
    c. Rates are lowest for Caucasian men.
    d. Rates are lowest for Pacific Islander women.

Black women don't crack

99. When experiencing mental health concerns, from whom are racial and ethnic minorities LEAST likely to seek help?

    a. A primary care physician
    b. A counselor
    c. Religious clergy
    d. A traditional healer

100. What is the GREATEST cultural barrier to receiving mental health treatment?

    a. The stigma of mental illness
    b. Mistrust of mental health providers
    c. Readily available alternatives (healers, clergy, etc.)
    d. A lack of family support

101. What do studies indicate about lesbian, gay, bisexual, and transgender (LGBT) individuals?

    a. They are more likely to abuse alcohol and drugs than the general population.
    b. They are similar to the general population in their use of alcohol and drugs.
    c. They are more likely to use drugs but not more likely to use alcohol than others.
    d. They are less likely to abuse alcohol and drugs than the general population.

102. What does the term *cultural brokering* refer to?

    a. Immigration and naturalization assistance
    b. Financial managers for ethnic and racial minorities
    c. Housing services for ethnic and racial minorities
    d. Liaison work between cultures to meet needs

103. How do the rates of heavy alcohol use among youth ages twelve to seventeen in rural areas compare?

    a. Double the rates in metropolitan areas
    b. Slightly higher than the rates in metropolitan areas
    c. About the same as the rates in metropolitan areas
    d. Half the rates found in metropolitan areas

104. Although homeless individuals are more likely to receive detoxification services than people not homeless, what percentage will receive full treatment for their alcohol or substance abuse problems?

    a. 15 percent
    b. 25 percent
    c. 35 percent
    d. 45 percent

105. Homeless individuals are particularly susceptible to substance abuse due to the stress and hopelessness of their current situation. What are the three most common substances of abuse among this population?

a. Alcohol, crack cocaine, and marijuana
b. Alcohol, opioids, and marijuana
c. Alcohol, opioids, and crack cocaine
d. Alcohol, marijuana, and inhalants

106. What is the case management model that seeks to identify clients' needs and assist clients in obtaining access various identified resources known as?

a. Brokerage or Generalist Model
b. Program of Assertive Community Treatment Model
c. Strengths-Based Perspective
d. Clinical or Rehabilitation Model

107. Which is the ONLY case management model that specifically addresses making contact with clients in their homes and other natural settings?

a. Clinical or Rehabilitation Model
b. Strengths-Based Perspective
c. Program of Assertive Community Treatment Model
d. Brokerage or Generalist Model

108. What is the case management approach that focuses on helping clients assert direct and personal control in the search for resources?

a. Program of Assertive Community Treatment Model
b. Clinical or Rehabilitation model
c. Brokerage or Generalist Model
d. Strengths-Based Perspective

109. What is the case management model that integrates therapeutic and resource acquisition activities known as?

a. Strengths-Based Perspective
b. Clinical or Rehabilitation Model
c. Brokerage or Generalist model
d. Program of Assertive Community Treatment Model

110. Among the numerous principles that are essential to effective case management, how is the principle of advocacy BEST described?

a. Taking the client's side in situations of conflict
b. Ensuring the client understands institutional rules
c. Helping an institution to meet a client's desires
d. Advocating for the client's best interests

72

111. How are the clinical, evaluative, and administrative activities that link clients with treatment, community services, and other resources needed to carry out a treatment plan MOST comprehensively referred to?

a. Case management
b. Client advocacy
c. Service coordination
d. Resource linkage

112. How is the individual who is responsible to carry out the clinical monitoring and collaborative client assessments, evaluations, referrals, treatment coordination, and goodness-of-fit appraisals of the treatment plan to client goals and objectives BEST known as?

a. Case manager
b. Service coordinator
c. Therapist
d. Administrator

113. A program or agency at times may require outside services to continue functioning properly. When an outside official or agency provides services solely to maintain the function and viability of a treating agency or program, confidentiality is maintained when service providers sign a

a. Contractual Agreement for Limited Services (CALS).
b. Qualified Service Organization Agreement (QSOA).
c. Confidentiality and Privacy Service Agreement (CPSA).
d. Consent and Disclosure Limitations Contract (CDLC).

114. What is a brief, but comprehensively integrated public health approach to early substance abuse intervention and treatment known as?

a. Treatment, Brief Intervention, Referral, and Screening (TBIRS)
b. Brief Intervention, Screening, Referral, and Treatment (BISRT)
c. Referral, Screening, Brief Intervention, and Treatment (RSBIT)
d. Screening, Brief Intervention, and Referral to Treatment (SBIRT)

115. What is the key feature that differentiates a substance abuse counselor who merely practices in the field from one who succeeds in changing clients' lives?

a. The knowledge of addiction issues
b. The ability to be empathetic
c. The skill to set clear boundaries
d. The capacity to firmly confront

116. A great deal is communicated nonverbally in the counseling process. How much communication does nonverbal body language account for, according to research?

a. 10 percent
b. 25 percent
c. 50 percent
d. 75 percent

117. During the intake process, it is important for clients to sign an informed consent form. Of the following, what is the MOST significant reason for signing this form?

a. To acquaint clients with program rules, regulations, and boundaries
b. To ensure full compliance with program accreditation standards
c. To better develop a meaningful treatment plan
d. To ensure client commitment to and readiness for treatment

118. The Substance Abuse and Mental Health Services Administration (SAMHSA) maintains a national registry known as NREPP. What does this acronym refer to?

a. National Registry of Examinations for Psychological Practices
b. National Registry of Excellence in Program Practicum
c. National Registry of Evidence-Based Programs and Practices
d. National Registry of Examiners for Program Procedures

119. It is important to determine a client's readiness for change at the outset of treatment. From among the following, what is the BEST indicator of readiness?

a. A client's statement of his or her readiness for change
b. The client and family's level of emotional and physical pain
c. The client and family's admission that there is a substance abuse problem
d. A client's changes in finances required to continue the substance abuse

120. Significant substance abuse can arrest personal progress and growth in many ways. How will emotional and other normal developmental stages MOST likely be affected?

a. They will progress more slowly due to significant substance abuse.
b. They will progress more rapidly due to significant substance abuse.
c. They will be largely skipped due to significant substance abuse.
d. They remain unchanged due to significant substance abuse.

121. The impact of substance abuse in the family varies based on the user's family position, role, age, and so on. What is one reason substance abuse in the family is NOT initiated or maintained?

a. The need to exert control over other family members
b. The need to produce a crisis to get any meaningful attention
c. The need to cope with severe depression or anxiety
d. The need to cope with unrealistic expectations

122. There are numerous methods used to encourage a substance abuser to enter treatment. Who carries out a programmed confrontation?

a. A trained addictions counselor
b. A primary care physician
c. A psychotherapist
d. A family member

123. Substance abuse takes a toll on all involved. How is community reinforcement training (CRT) used?

a. To assist a substance user to reduce his or her level of use
b. To keep drug use paraphernalia clean and disease free
c. To motivate a substance user to enter a treatment program
d. To persuade heroin users not to share needles with others

124. Motivating an addict to enter treatment is often difficult. Which treatment entry method uses the intervention network as part of its motivational process?

    a. The Johnson Method
    b. Community reinforcement training (CRT)
    c. The ARISE Method
    d. The community reinforcement approach (CRA)

125. Families have much to offer the treatment process. Beyond client abstinence, what is the main goal of involving the family in treatment?

    a. To corner an addict into making changes by escalating family pressure
    b. To help the family to better cope with the client's addictive behaviors and the related consequences
    c. To teach the family about the biological processes that underlie addiction
    d. To educate the family about substance abuse as a chronic disorder requiring lifelong changes

126. There are numerous reasons for not involving the family in treatment. Who are the family members MOST likely to participate in treatment?

    a. Adult children
    b. Adult siblings
    c. Adult women
    d. Adult men

127. There are many approaches and techniques that may be used to help families understand addiction and support sobriety. How does the Bowen family systems theory view the family?

    a. An interdependent emotional unit
    b. Autonomous members in a collective
    c. Functional co-participants in limited endeavors
    d. Disparate participants seeking harmony

128. When helping families adjust to and maintain in-home sobriety, what is the therapeutic intervention that draws upon extended support linkages to produce motivation and reinforcement known as?

    a. Structural or strategic systems therapy
    b. Network therapy
    c. Cognitive-behavioral therapy
    d. Multidimensional family therapy

129. Many therapeutic approaches might be helpful in working with families of addicts. Of those commonly used, which brief therapeutic approach uses the miracle question technique?

    a. Cognitive-behavioral therapy
    b. Bowen family systems therapy
    c. Multidimensional family therapy
    d. Solution-focused family therapy

130. Genetic factors can play a significant role in an individual's susceptibility to substance abuse and addiction. It is estimated that genetic factors account for

    a. 20 to 40 percent of addiction vulnerability.
    b. 30 to 50 percent of addiction vulnerability.
    c. 40 to 60 percent of addiction vulnerability.
    d. 50 to 70 percent of addiction vulnerability.

131. Numerous factors have protective influences against the development of substance abuse and addiction. If the home itself is a high-risk environment (parental drug use, etc.), how can a minor's healthy development be optimized?

    a. They distance themselves from their dysfunctional families.
    b. They develop a talent, skill, or something valued by others.
    c. They do neither A nor B.
    d. They do both A and B.

132. How is the concept of resilience, from the perspective of mental health, BEST described?

    a. Internal strengths necessary to cope with challenging events
    b. Adequate resources to draw upon in times of emotional compromise
    c. Social networks that can offer support during times of distress
    d. Intellectual fund of information to reason and cope well with problems

133. Culture can play a significant role in substance abuse. How do Hispanic and Latino populations, in general, tend to respond to alcohol problems in the family?

    a. By lashing out and aggressively confronting the drinking problem
    b. By attempting to ignore and avoid discussing the drinking problem
    c. By seeking out authority figures to help them engage the drinking problem
    d. By seeking out religious leaders to help them engage the drinking problem

134. African Americans have a significant presence in the United States. What is the percentage of the population that identifies themselves as black?

    a. 8 percent
    b. 11 percent
    c. 13 percent
    d. 16 percent

135. Native Americans (American Indians and Alaska natives) have distinct cultures, particularly among those living on reservations or trust lands. What percentage report alcohol use?

    a. 15 percent
    b. 25 percent
    c. 35 percent
    d. 20 percent

136. The racial mix of the United States continues to shift substantially. What is the fastest-growing minority group in the nation?

    a. Hispanics and Latinos
    b. Asians and Pacific Islanders
    c. African Americans
    d. Native Americans

137. Sooner or later, all treatment programs end, and a discharge summary and continuing care plan will then be required. What is the key difference between a discharge summary and a continuing care plan?

    a. A discharge plan provides directions for further treatment, while the continuing care plan addresses the client's clinical presentation at discharge.

    b. A discharge plan provides an overview of treatment and outcomes, while the continuing care plan addresses aftercare options based on the client's response to treatment.

    c. A discharge plan provides a roster of prior professionals involved, while the continuing care plan proposes further professionals to engage in the treatment process.

    d. A discharge plan provides a theoretical orientation to a client's presentation, while a continuing care plan offers a model for further intervention.

138. Tracking client progress longitudinally is important to measure progress and document program effectiveness. How often is client data typically reviewed?

    a. Annually

    b. Biannually

    c. Semiannually

    d. Quarterly

139. Ideally, a treatment plan should be developed with which of the following sets of people?

    a. A consultant and the primary counselor

    b. The primary counselor and an assigned treatment team member

    c. The counselor and the client together

    d. A program administrator and a consultant

140. Treatment plans should refer to the type of program service modality being offered. Which of the following is NOT a common modality?

    a. Residential

    b. Outpatient

    c. Scholastic

    d. Perinatal

141. Fundamental ethical principles govern the addiction treatment process, especially in situations of medication-assisted treatment (MAT) for opioid addiction. What does the principle of nonmaleficence refer to?

    a. Preserving client autonomy

    b. Working to a client's benefit

    c. Doing no harm to a client

    d. Faithfully honoring commitments

142. The capacity to be empathetic is important in counseling. What must a counselor do when relating to clients over issues of their past?

    a. Avoid any kind of emotional connection that compromises objectivity.

    b. Avoid becoming overly drawn into the client's history and issues.

    c. Ensure total emersion in the client's issues to properly relate and understand.

    d. Ensure every detail of past pain and trauma is relieved and released.

143. The counselor–client relationship can be very complex. What does the term *transference* refer to?

    a. Feelings from the client that the counselor uses to strengthen the relationship
    b. Feelings from the counselor that the client accepts to grow and improve
    c. Feelings from a past relationship that are projected onto the counselor
    d. Feelings from current relationships that are added to the counseling experience

144. The therapeutic relationship can produce feelings that are challenging. What does the term *countertransference* refer to?

    a. Feelings from the client that are projected onto the counselor
    b. Feelings from the counselor that are projected onto the client
    c. Feelings that the client openly shares with the counselor
    d. Feelings from the counselor that are used to promote resolution

145. Working with substance-abusing clients can result in a variety of emotive experiences. What does the term *secondary trauma* refer to?

    a. The overlay of emotional abuse in a physically abusive relationship
    b. The medical sequelae that may arise after years of emotional abuse
    c. Entering a relationship with abusive features like those experienced before
    d. Symptoms in the counselor emerging from high exposure to client traumas

146. Substance-abusing clients can be clinically and personally challenging. Of what is compassion fatigue a key symptom?

    a. Counselor burnout
    b. Clients with high-abuse histories
    c. Counselor apathy
    d. Clients with multimodal issues

147. What does a treatment frame assist both the counselor and clients to establish and maintain?

    a. An effective theoretical orientation
    b. Healthy boundaries in treatment
    c. Shared meanings and definitions
    d. An effective treatment focus

148. Trust is an essential component of a productive counseling relationship. Which of the following is NOT a key counselor contribution to the development of trust?

    a. Unconditional positive regard
    b. Nonjudgmental attitudes
    c. Greater latitude in boundary setting
    d. Ongoing commitment to client success

149. Counselor–client relationships can at times become inappropriately intimate and intense. What is one particularly problematic potential from this?

    a. Client rejection of the counselor
    b. Client romantic feelings for a counselor
    c. Client apathy regarding a counselor
    d. Client feelings of anger toward a counselor

150. Clients with a history of sexual abuse may have poor boundaries with others. If a counselor becomes sexually involved with a client, what are the consequences?

a. Termination of employment
b. Loss of licensure
c. Potential prosecution
d. All of the above

Answers and Explanations

1. A: Opioids (heroin, morphine, codeine, etc.) and the semisynthetic and synthetic derivatives have a withdrawal syndrome generally characterized by nausea, vomiting, runny nose, watery eyes, chills, abdominal cramps, anorexia, weakness, bone pains, tremors, sweating, feelings of panic, and persistent yawning. More serious symptoms such as convulsions and cardiovascular collapse are very rare. Hallucinogenics and psychedelics typically do not have a withdrawal syndrome, though flashbacks of past trips may well occur. Barbiturate withdrawal symptoms include: insomnia, anxiety, delirium and tremors, and the possibility of convulsions (seizures) and death. Benzodiazepine withdrawal symptoms are similar to those of barbiturate withdrawal but potentially at least somewhat less severe.

2. C: Studies reveal that major factors in drug abuse vulnerability include social, family, culture, and other factors. However, epidemiological studies reveal that genetic factors contribute as much as half of an individual's risk for drug abuse. The role of genetics is slightly higher for males than females, and the role of genetics in heroin abuse exceeds that of any other drug. Further, the greater and more severe the manifestation of drug abuse, the more predominant the role of genetics in the predisposition for substance abuse. Theorists suggest a malfunction in neurotransmitter production results in a potentially profound need to self-medicate to compensate.

3. C: There are numerous factors that contribute to the tendency of adolescents to impulsiveness, unruly behavior, and risk taking. These include limited life experience, high energy, a concomitant desire for external stimuli and engagement, a predisposition toward peer influences, and so on. Of primary influence, however, is the issue of neurological immaturity. Key portions of the brain that manage judgment and emotional control are among the last to mature. The prefrontal cortex, where impulse control, reasoning, and foresight are managed, does not mature until early adulthood. Further, the adolescent brain appears to be more receptive to the effects of substances of abuse as well as more vulnerable to subsequent physiological consequences.

4. C: Depressant drugs reduce levels of stress-related neurotransmitters and inhibit stress-accelerating hormones (e.g., adrenalin and cortisol). This is accomplished, in part, by mimicking the body's three natural stress-reducing analgesics known as endorphins (a contraction of the term *endogenous morphine*). Lacking symptoms of stress, depressant abusers such as heroin users may use the drug infrequently for years without developing an addiction. Should significant stress arise, however, the abuse of depressant drugs becomes highly likely. It is further theorized that addiction potential is enhanced where biological factors may make stress susceptibility greater.

5. B: Benzodiazepine tolerance develops fairly rapidly. Consequently, anxiety cannot be treated effectively beyond four months, regardless of the dosage. Polydrug use is particularly problematic as using benzodiazepines in conjunction with pain medications, alcohol, and antihistamines can produce severe respiratory depression and even death. In the United States, the second-leading cause of drug-related emergency department admission is benzodiazepine overdose. Due to the development of tolerance, even after use for as little as two to three weeks, individuals must be weaned away from benzodiazepines under medical supervision, most commonly over a period of months.

6. A: Low-dose ingestion of alcohol has stimulant effects, producing euphoria and excitability. This occurs as a result of low-dose alcohol triggering the brain's the dopaminergic reward pathway. At higher doses, alcohol is a powerful central nervous system depressant, producing drowsiness and sedation. Very high levels can induce stupor, coma, and even death. Body weight and food intake can substantially affect blood alcohol levels and absorption rates. Food can slow absorption, and body weight can dilute the alcohol taken in. Age, however, can play a meaningful role as well. The elderly have less lean body mass and muscle and more fat. Nonfat body mass contains water, which dilutes alcohol; alcohol is not soluble in fat. Thus, the elderly become intoxicated more readily than younger individuals of their same height and weight.

7. C: Virtually all drugs that cross the blood–brain barrier will affect the fetus, and fetal addiction can result, requiring suffering withdrawals at birth. However, of all drugs of abuse, alcohol is the most dangerous to the developing fetus. Even moderate drinking during pregnancy (particularly during the first three months) can result in birth defects such as organ and skeletal malformations and intellectual impairment. Some babies appear normal at birth and subsequently develop serious learning and behavioral problems as they grow older. More regular alcohol abuse may result in fetal alcohol syndrome (FAS), often with characteristic head and facial deformities, mental retardation, heart defects, stunted growth, and so on. When the typical facial characteristics are lacking, the disorder is called fetal alcohol effects.

8. B: In most people, monoamine oxidases (MAOs) regulate the levels of serotonin, dopamine, and norepinephrine. Those with an excess of MAO may experience endogenous depression due to reduced key neurotransmitter levels. These individuals appear to self-medicate by using stimulant drugs. Their goal is to lift depression, increase energy, and reduce inward tension. Other people with unique genetic dopamine receptor variations may be particularly susceptible to addiction due to their tendency toward impulsivity, anger, agitation, and boredom. Many in this group are drawn to high-risk activities such as extreme sports as well as drug abuse. For this group, stimulants are uniquely rewarding and thus profoundly compelling and addictive.

9. D: Whether snorted, injected, or smoked (oral ingestion is not effective), cocaine triggers the release of dopamine, serotonin, and norepinephrine. The primary effect occurs through the buildup of dopamine, though all neurotransmitters involved contribute to the subsequent euphoria. Not only does cocaine stimulate the release of these key neurotransmitters, but it also blocks their natural reabsorption by inhibiting a reuptake transporter from carrying out its normal functions. After the euphoria passes, neurotransmitter depletion induces a sense of profound dysphoria and depression, thus generating a need for further use of the drug. Individuals who are naturally deficient in serotonin appear to be particularly at risk for cocaine addiction.

10. A: Nootropics are drugs designed to boost cognitive performance. These neuro-enhancing drugs tend to be used by highly competitive and overcommitted individuals to enhance concentration, focus, and memory and to help ward off fatigue and somnolence. Among the more popular of these medications are Provigil (generic: mondafinil) and Adderall (generic: dextroamphetamine saccharate, amphetamine aspartate, dextroamphetamine sulfate, and amphetamine sulfate—or, sometimes, just amphetamine/dextroamphetamine). Adderall contains amphetamine salts designed to increase dopamine and norepinephrine levels in the brain and is used in the treatment of attention deficit hyperactivity disorder (ADHD). Provigil is a stimulant used in the treatment of sleep disorders. Another nootropic, Piracetam (or Nootrapil; generic: 2-oxo-1-pyrrolidine acetamide), is sold as a supplement. Used widely in Europe, it has not received Food and Drug Administration (FDA) approval. Chemically, it influences neuronal and vascular functions and thereby enhances cognitive function without acting as a sedative or stimulant. It has been used to treat depression, the disabling effects of stroke, and a variety of other neurological disorders.

11. B: Use of alcohol early in the day, including a first drink to cope with a hangover, is one symptom in the progression to the heavy drinking stage. The first stage in the development of alcoholism is social drinking. These individuals drink for enjoyment and relaxation and remain within the conventions of expected use and behavior. Many individuals rarely, if ever, step outside this category of drinking. Most who do find the trigger to be unexpected or unusually burdensome stress. With the onset of a sufficient stressor, some individuals will progress to the second stage of heavy drinking. In this stage, drinkers violate norms and expected alcohol use behaviors and begin to experience negative consequences. If heavy drinking continues, drinkers enter the final stage of dependent drinking, characterized by out-of-control drinking and obsession with the use of alcohol. High-functioning alcoholics (HFA) are able to compartmentalize their alcohol use and thereby function well socially, though poorly privately and intimately.

12. D: The five stages in the life cycle of heroin addiction consist of the following: (1) experimentation—dabbling in many drugs, including snorting or subcutaneous heroin injection; (2) initiation—a typically unpleasant first experience (nausea and vomiting) followed by increasingly enjoyable subsequent injections; (3) commitment—assuming the identity of the heroin subculture and orienting life toward habit maintenance; (4) disjunction—crime, arrests, imprisonment, court-ordered treatment, and efforts to reduce the habit to a more manageable extent or to deal with physical illness and compromise; (5) maturation—phasing out drugs (usually at an age closer to forty than twenty, though potentially into the fifties or sixties) or dying from the abuse.

13. C: The first step toward cocaine abuse begins with experimental use. Most relationships are with nonusers, and no apparent consequences from experimentation are observed. The second stage is compulsive use. In this stage, cocaine is used to cope with depression, mood swings and stress and to cope with coming down from a desirable high. The number of friends who use increases, and nonuser friends begin to be avoided. Financial problems begin to appear. The third and final stage, dysfunctional use, is characterized by preoccupation with the use of the drug, chronic sleep and health problems, serious disruptions in social and family life, and work and financial devastation. Treatment may be sought as the consequences mount and the compulsion to use becomes overwhelming. Trading sex for drugs is common, lending to high-risk of exposure to sexually transmitted infections (STIs).

14. B and C: Weak family ties lead to a loss of normally internalized behavioral and decision-making restraints. Feelings of familial estrangement lend to poor family and community socialization and an absence of prosocial constructs. Highly chaotic, disorganized, and disadvantaged communities are particularly lacking in the ability to exert positive, conforming influences and to create broader community ties and commitment. Weak societal ties result in a loss of obligation to the community and society at large. External restraints are then reduced or removed entirely when closer ties are made with individuals espousing and living the norms of a drug subculture. In such circumstances, the usual restraints of social disapproval and fear of punishment are bypassed as the subcultural norms replace and obviate those of the usually prevailing broader social structure. In overly affluent communities, absent, neglectful, and emotionally unavailable adults leave their youth unduly susceptible to peer pressure, consumerism, and hedonistic pursuits, including drug use and abuse. Thus, in both disadvantaged and affluent communities, weak family and societal ties can lead to substance abuse issues.

15. D: Anabolic steroids are typically used for their muscle-enhancing benefits. This produces an aspect of psychological dependence as individuals use them to achieve social benefits—to look better and to sustain enhanced athletic prowess, and so on. Issues of tolerance to the drug lead to higher dosages over time. At both medical and higher doses, anabolic steroids can induce significant euphoria. It appears that steroids engage both opioid and dopamine neurotransmission systems in the brain. In consequence, the use of opiates to deal with overexertion pain can more readily lead to opiate addiction as well. Anabolic steroid addictive potential appears on a par with caffeine, nicotine, and the benzodiazepines. Symptoms of withdrawal are very much like those experienced by cocaine users, including insomnia, anorexia, headaches, restlessness, poor libido, and dysphoria. Depressive symptoms can be significant enough to approach suicidality. Appropriate titration and weaning may be required to manage issues of withdrawal.

16. C: Individuals present for treatment for a great variety of reasons. Among these are: (1) a need for transient relief from the effects of their substance abuse but still intending to return; (2) a desire to modify their substance abuse but recognizing only mildly associated problems from the abuse; (3) a primary desire to maintain employment, a marriage, physical health, mental health, or for other situationally driven reasons; (4) ambivalent feelings about their substance abuse and unsure what they really want; (5) a genuine desire to change but with a sense of fear that they will be unable to produce the commitment needed to fully realize it; and so on. Determining where client readiness for change is crucial to producing a treatment approach that can optimize his or her potential for ultimate success.

17. C: Client ambivalence about substance abuse is natural and unavoidable. If this ambivalence is misinterpreted to be denial, resistance, or confrontation, the counselor–client relationship may become unnecessarily conflicted and polarized. Indeed, common motivational conflicts include: (1) pre-contemplation—"I'm not concerned, but others in my life will feel reassured if we talk"; (2) contemplation—"Stopping drug use might help me feel better about myself, but I still can't see never using again"; (3) preparation—"I'll set a quit date, but I don't know if I am strong enough to follow through"; (4) action—"I've been sober for three weeks, and now my old self wants to celebrate by getting high"; (5) maintenance—"After months of sobriety, I still sometimes wonder if total abstinence is really required."

18. B: This primary goal is best realized by reviewing and evaluating symptoms, the current situation, available resources, amenability to treatment, readiness for change, program goodness of fit, possible dual diagnoses, potential referral needs, and so on. During screening and intake evaluation, a great many things will be learned, but all information should primarily be used to determine an optimum initial course of intervention and treatment, given the client's characteristics and needs. There may be situations where client characteristics require referral to another treatment provided, but merely off-loading difficult clients should never be a goal of the screening process. Medical needs, in particular, may necessitate hospitalization, inpatient detoxification, or referral to a program setting with a higher level of care or with the capacity to better evaluate and treat certain dual diagnoses. Otherwise, however, screening should remain focused on designing a treatment program that will optimize the client's potential for eventual success.

19. B: Intake screening tools are designed to identify those clients requiring a more thorough assessment in targeted matters of concern. In substance abuse, this involves screening for the presence of a pattern of use worthy of concern, an outright disorder requiring treatment, or the likely presence of co-occurring disorders (CODs), such as possible underlying mental illness, that should also be assessed further. Screening tools are not typically designed to define any particular mental disorder but rather the likelihood that a co-occurring mental disorder may exist. Screeners should be familiar with specific protocols for properly scoring screening instruments as well as protocols for specific steps to take when an individual breaches the cutoff threshold for substance abuse or a co-occurring mental disorder.

20. D: Individuals with substance use disorders also run a much higher risk of eventual death by suicide. Indeed, those who inject drugs run a risk fourteen times higher than those in the general population. Of further importance, individuals in treatment continue to run a substantially elevated risk of suicide, thus treatment staff should be continuously aware of indicators of cascading risk (e.g., ideation, gestures, isolation, mood changes, etc.). The risk of suicide in treatment typically arises from factors concurrent with the decision to enter treatment. Specially: (1) they typically enter treatment when circumstances are out of control; (b) treatment is usually accepted in the face of multiple other life crises (job, marriage, health, etc.); and (3) seeking treatment often coincides with peak periods of concurrent depression.

21. C: Screening is a process of examining a client for one or more specific potential problems, while assessment defines the nature and extent of the problem and offers treatment recommendations. Assessment involves a clinical evaluation of client functioning and presenting well-being. A basic assessment includes fundamental information gathering and examination of client problems, strengths, disabilities, co-occurring disorders, and readiness for change. Co-occurring disorders (CODs) are obtained via referral to a qualified health care professional (licensed clinical social worker, psychologist, psychiatrist, etc.). Once formalized, relevant aspects of CODs are integrated into the treatment plan formulation and application.

22. D: It is important to identify and measure the changing nature of every client's status as related to issues of addiction and any other co-occurring mental illness. Only by tracking change over time is it possible to determine the effectiveness of the treatments being provided as well as the degree of the client's continuing commitment to change. Objective measurement tools include: Addiction Severity Index (ASI), Mental Health Screening Form-III, Symptom Distress Scale (SDS), and University of Rhode Island Change Assessment Scale (URICA).

23. D: There is no single gold standard assessment tool for the identification of co-occurring disorders (CODs). Rather, it is important for the counselor to be able screen for CODs and then select one or more appropriate assessment tools by which to more extensively assess the presence or absence of a true COD. Consequently, depression might be assessed using the twenty-one-question Beck Depression Inventory (BDI), and a standardized mental status examination (MSE) may be required to explore possible thought disorders and other potential mental functioning irregularities (e.g., hallucinations, delusions, suicidality, etc.). In concert with this, careful attention to corollaries between substances abused and mental functioning changes, particularly during extended periods of abstinence, can aid in determining whether or not mental disorders are actually transient sequelae from substances abuse or true underlying disorders.

24. D: Obtaining information from collateral contacts is an essential step in the twelve-step assessment process required for investigating primary and co-occurring disorders (CODs). Clients may minimize, omit, alter, or otherwise revise information crucial to the assessment. By making collateral contacts, the likelihood of incomplete, skewed, or outright fabricated information is greatly reduced. The full twelve-step assessment process includes: (1) engaging the client; (2) making collateral contacts (with proper client authorization); (3) screening for CODs; (4) assessing substance use and mental disorder severity; (5) identifying the optimal care setting (e.g., day treatment, outpatient, inpatient, etc.); (6) establishing the diagnosis; (7) identifying impairments and disabilities; (8) determining strengths and supports; (9) determining any special language or cultural needs and supports; (10) determining other problem areas (health, finances, education, etc.); (11) identifying readiness for change; and (12) treatment planning.

25. A: Intake is focused on fundamental information gathering as opposed to exploring feelings, attitudes, and readiness for change. After basic information has been gathered, intake information can be extended and augmented by the use of objective measurement tools such as: (1) the Addiction Severity Index (ASI), the Mental Health Screening Form-III, the Symptom Distress Scale (SDS), and the University of Rhode Island Change Assessment Scale (URICA). Once this information has been assembled, the counselor must organize it in such a way that all meaningful findings can be integrated into the treatment planning and intervention process.

26. B: The Substance Abuse Subtle Screening Inventory (SASSI) has been extensively researched and revised. Now in its third edition (SASSI-3), it is composed of both obvious and subtle items. This makes it particularly useful in situations where individuals are either unwilling or unable to acknowledge substance abuse problems. It is comprised of sixty-seven true–false items as well as a twenty-six-item self-report section on substance use and takes less than fifteen minutes to complete. Designed clinical use, it is not appropriate for preemployment screening or other nonclinical applications. The Michigan Alcohol Screening Test (MAST) is one of the oldest and most accurate alcohol screening tests available, but it offers no special tools for ferreting out issues of truth. The Screening, Brief Intervention, and Referral to Treatment (SBIRT) is a quick and simple tool for identifying those who use substances at at-risk levels and those already experiencing substance use issues. However, it offers no special tools for circumventing compromised truth telling. The Addiction Severity Index (ASI) is not a screening tool but a tool for assessment and treatment planning.

27. A: Measures of client's compliance are derived through the treatment process, not through the screening or assessment processes. Key screening and assessment outcomes include: (1) positive client engagement; (2) essential authorizations and consents for treatment and collateral contacts; (3) diagnosis and severity of substance abuse and related co-occurring disorders; (4) the proper level of care (inpatient vs. outpatient, etc.); (5) pertinent disabilities and functional impairments; (6) understanding of client strengths and available supports; (7) cultural or linguistic needs and resources; (8) other unique problems related to health, housing, education and vocational training, cognitive capacity, social needs, and spiritual needs.

28. C: The presence or absence of a substance or alcohol abuse problem is determined during the screening process, not during the assessment process. During assessment, the presence of a problem is refined to reveal the nature of the problem, its diagnosis, and its extent and severity. Key goals and purposes of assessment include: (1) substance abuse history; (2) the severity and extent of the presenting substance or alcohol abuse problem; (3) co-occurring mental disorders; (4) legal issues that may contribute to or impede the treatment process (e.g., court-ordered treatment vs. detention or work-release issues, severe financial burdens of fines and court costs, etc.); (5) health problems and stability for treatment; (6) available resources to help resolve the problem (family, social, employment-related, etc.); (7) client strengths, maturity, motivation, and readiness for treatment; and (8) the ideal treatment approach for optimal odds of success.

29. D: Treatment planning communications with clients (and involved significant others) must be appropriate to age and developmental level to ensure optimal comprehension and commitment. Counselors must also be sensitive to issues of race, ethnicity, and culture. Indeed, these issues may, at times, be paramount for successful treatment. For example, substance abuse in some instances may be culturally sanctioned (or rejected harshly), and racial or ethnic tensions or disparities may at times become barriers to successful treatment. Finally, communications must be free of technical jargon and obscure acronyms. This may be difficult for some professionals as treatment providers at times utilize professionally obscure wording and references that have become common to them.

30. C: When clients understand the data and findings from the assessment, they more fully understand what challenges they face and the importance and value of the interventions being selected. Client buy-in to the treatment plan is essential to its optimum success. Therefore, assessment findings need to be thoroughly explained and clearly related to proposed treatments in words and ways that meet the communication style and patterns of the client and his or her significant others (involved family, friends, etc.). Sharing with significant others is important so that they may better offer the client effective support and to avoid unintentionally undermining treatment efforts. In sharing this information, feedback should be elicited from the client and involved others to ensure their full understanding of the available information and of the treatment processes and purposes. Feedback can also ensure that all intake and assessment information was accurately obtained and properly recorded.

31. A: Historically, clients have been provided bundled services in a one-size-fits-all approach that was not individualized. Newer research reveals that unbundling services to pick and choose those most appropriate for the client is far better. Therefore, the client assessment process should not only identify client needs but client preferences as well. With this information, a treatment plan should be formulated to meets both the client's needs and preferences. Subsequently, the client's needs and preferences should be optimally matched with available resources, intervention types, level of care, and service intensity. Doing so not only increases client retention in the treatment program but improves the overall success of the treatment provided. In this way, treatment outcomes can be optimized for treatment success.

32. C: Patient placement criteria (PPC) provide guidelines for the conditions required for substance abuse treatment admission (admission criteria), criteria for continuing treatment at each designated level of care (continuing care criteria), and the criteria that must guide client movement between various levels of care or release from a given treatment program or facility (discharge and transfer criteria). Overall, PPC standards address appropriate treatment settings and facilities, staffing levels and the skill mix, and the requisite kinds of services for treatments at any given level of care. The guidelines are based on specific areas of client assessment, including relevant substance abuse diagnoses.

33. B: The clients most ready for change are those who perceive the need for help with the process of change and particularly when other options are perceived as comparatively less attractive. Further, treatment program retention appears to be closely related to a client's perceptions of his or her substance abuse problem as well as the extent of understanding of available treatment options. Readiness is compromised when other nontreatment alternatives seem acceptable and when the client has significant feelings of ambivalence about the need for change. In situations of high ambivalence or where the client is a nonvoluntary participant, the engagement or creation of a motivational crisis may assist him or her in becoming more accepting of treatment.

34. D: Treatment sequencing ensures a continuum of care and treatment will be prioritized in such a way as to meet a client's most basic needs before less-fundamental needs are addressed. This typically requires a case management care model, which offers a coordinated approach to service delivery. Case management requires a holistic approach, ensuring that not only substance abuse issues are addressed but that physical and mental health and spiritual and social needs are also being adequately evaluated and met throughout the treatment process. This requires five key evaluative and engagement processes: (1) assessment, (2) planning, (3) linkage (especially when multidisciplinary or even outside services needed), (4) monitoring (including documentation), and (5) advocacy.

35. A: Abraham Maslow proposed the Hierarchy of Needs in 1943, which has become a foundational understanding in psychology. The concept indicates that an individual's needs are prioritized in importance, with more basic needs such as survival, security, and sociality holding higher order importance than love, belonging, self-esteem, purpose, and self-actualization. An understanding of this paradigm is important in treatment planning. Specifically, if basic survival and safety needs remain unmet, efforts to meet other needs will not elicit a sense of optimal responsiveness and wholeness from the client. This incongruence can negatively affect the treatment of the substance disorder as well.

36. C: Abraham Maslow's Hierarchy of Needs has been presented in varying ways but essentially includes the following: (1) physiological needs (basic needs for survival); (2) security needs (safety and protection as a family and society); (3) love and belonging needs (social needs such as friendship, love, appreciation, etc.); (4) esteem needs (self-respect, recognition as unique, personal value, etc.); (5) the need for purpose (meaning to life, finding and meeting one's inner potential, etc.); (6) self-actualization (creativity, morality, wisdom, etc.). Until lower-order needs are met, it is difficult to invest in or even fully appreciate higher-order needs. Substance abuse transiently obviates any awareness of needs and at times even artificially substitutes for them (feelings of well-being, status, creativity, etc.). Consequently, until substantial progress is made in meeting hierarchical needs, problems with extinguishing substance abuse are likely to persist.

37. D: How the clinician asks questions can make a substantial difference. For example, the general question "Are you depressed?" can easily be denied outright (based upon a sense of negative judgment) or misunderstood (if the client does not understand precisely what the clinician is asking). Clearer and more specific clinical questioning might be: "Do you feel sad, hopeless, too tired, or have problems concentrating?" Open-ended questioning is good as it allows the client to answer freely and broadly. However, leading questions are not helpful, even if open-ended in nature (i.e., "You're not feeling depressed, are you?"). Finally, professional jargon may make a clinician feel proficient and empowered, but it leaves clients confused and feeling vulnerable. It is always important to speak in easily understood terms.

38. D: A psychiatrist, George Engel, coined the term *biopsychosocial* in 1977 to support the interrelated and interconnected causal factors necessary to explain mental health disorders. The Biopsychosocial Model is widely used in the substance abuse field as it offers a more comprehensive way of explaining the numerous elements that contribute to developing and sustaining an addiction disorder. Use of this model allows for the concurrent application of numerous different theories and interventions, thereby offering a more comprehensive treatment approach. A unique strength of this model is that no single theory or intervention is necessarily superior to any other. In this way, differing views are seen as complementary and meaningful, even while highlighting the differences necessary to adequately identify and address the treatment complexity in managing multiple disorders.

39. B: The Chemical Use, Abuse, and Dependence (CUAD) Scale is used in substance abuse assessment, and it does derive a *Diagnostic and Statistical Manual of Mental Disorders (*DSM) diagnosis of substance use disorder. It is relatively brief (a five- to thirty-minute interview, depending on the degree and kinds of substances used) and it also requires limited training. However, it is best known for its utility in assessing substance abuse in mentally ill clients. It has most commonly been studied in clients with depression and schizophrenia, thus its applicability in other populations (e.g., bipolar disorder, etc.) is less well documented. It is a dependable and valid diagnostic instrument for determining the extent of substance abuse. The CUAD uses a short, partly structured interview that is far less time-consuming than earlier assessment methods such as the Addiction Severity Index (ASI). Researchers have confirmed the CUAD's accuracy.

40. D: The Symptom Checklist-90-R (SCL-90-R) is used to assess a broad range of psychological problems and key symptoms of psychopathology. The instrument is also used to measure client progress or treatment outcomes. Containing only ninety items and a five-point rating scale, the SCL-90-R can be completed in as little as twelve to fifteen minutes. Normed for individuals ages thirteen and older, the test produces an overview of symptoms and associated intensity at a specific point in time. The nine primary symptom dimensions measured are: somatization, obsessive-compulsive, interpersonal sensitivity, depression, anxiety, hostility, phobic anxiety, paranoid ideation, and psychoticism. The index of symptom severity facilitates treatment decisions and identifies problems before they become acute. The Global Severity Index serves as a summary. The reliability and validity of the instrument have been confirmed in more than 1,000 separate studies.

41. D: The COPES is used to measure the actual, preferred, and expected treatment environment or social climate of community treatment programs. These include residential facilities, rehabilitation centers, halfway houses, and care homes. COPES draws upon the opinions of both clients and staff using three key dimensions: (1) relationship dimensions, (2) personal growth dimensions, and (3) system maintenance dimensions. The relationship dimensions are assessed via three subscales: (1) involvement, (2) support, and (3) spontaneity. Four subscales are used to evaluate the personal growth dimensions: (1) autonomy, (2) practical orientation, (3) personal problems orientation, and (4) anger and aggression. The system maintenance dimensions are assessed via three subscales: (1) order and organization, (2) program clarity, and (3) staff control. Research reveals that these dimensions are directly related to objective indicators of treatment outcome such as drop-out rate, release rate, and community tenure. The regular use of COPES can lead to important program and service outcome measures and indices of program and service progress.

42. C: The Treatment Services Review (TSR) is designed for use in conjunction with the Addiction Severity Index (ASI). The TSR is a ten-minute structured interview that assesses the nature and frequency of treatment services provided for a client in the following domains: (1) medical problems; (2) substance use (alcohol and drug) problems; (3) employment and support problems; (4) family problems; (5) legal problems; and (6) psychological or emotional problems. Each domain is comprised of three sections. The first section reports the number of days that a target behavior or problem occurred. The second section records the number of times (per week) that a professional has provided services. The third section captures the number of structured sessions that were held for a particular problem during the prior week—whether through the index treatment program (in-program) or by others (out-program). The TSR provides a continuous record of the number and types of services provided, the rate at which these identified problems show change, and measures cost-effectiveness among the patient population that actually receives the services.

43. C: The behavior component of BIRP progress recording is focused on counselor observations and client statements. It begins with subjective data (the client's observations, thoughts, and direct quotes) and moves to objective data (counselor observations of client affect, mood, appearance, etc.). The intervention section captures the counselor's efforts toward goals and objectives (counselor understandings and working hypotheses, etc., general session content, whether homework was reviewed, e.g., journal, reading assignments, etc., if any) and the goals and objectives addressed this session. Response refers to the client's intervention response and treatment plan goals and objectives progress. Plan involves documentation of what is to happen next, goals and objectives revisions, scheduled activities (sessions, group work, etc.), and any new or updated interventions.

44. B: The chief complaint is the presenting problem or any significant issues requiring primary attention. History is any relevant historical information—deep history at intake or recent history as relevant to the chief complaint or presenting problem. Exam is any change or lack of change in mental status (MMSE), mood, and behavior—current appearance, speech changes, psychomotor (agitated or retarded), mood or affect (in client's words), observed expressions and emotive range, thought content and processes, insight, judgment, and impulse control. Assessment is any positive diagnostic studies, medication issues, or consultation summaries, along with comments from other service providers; five axes diagnoses; and a brief statement of overall impression. The plan is justification for any changes in the treatment plan and ongoing interventions, medication changes, or program changes, placement considerations, and so on, with the rationale for each.

45. A: The acronym SIGECAPS is a tool prompting the full evaluation of the symptoms of depression. Each letter addresses one of the key potential features of depression: sleep (any significant increase or decrease), interests (decrease or loss of interest in previously pleasurable activities or events), guilt (feelings of guilt and burden without any real culpability or feelings that are disproportionate to actual circumstances), energy (decreased energy or feelings of listlessness, weariness or fatigue), concentration (decreased ability to focus and cognitively pursue thoughts in a meaningful way), appetite (increased or decreased appetite, as evidenced by weight loss or weight gain), psychomotor agitation or retardation (jittery tension and agitation or lethargy and sluggishness in movements), and suicidal ideation (persistent thoughts of self-harm, potentially escalating into increasingly detailed plans over time).

46. C: Both of these formats were originated Roget and Johnson. CART refers to client condition (presentation, presenting problem, chief complaint, etc.), actions (actions the counselor did in response to the client's condition, response (client response to the actions or intervention), and treatment plan (how the response informs, extends, or clarifies the treatment plan). CHART refers to client condition (presentation, presenting problem, chief complaint, etc.), historical significance (of the client's condition), actions (actions taken by the counselor in response to the client's condition), response (client response to the actions or intervention), and treatment plan (how the client's response informs, extends, modifies, or clarifies the treatment plan).

47. A: A full biopsychosocial assessment should reveal specific client needs, strengths, weaknesses, and readiness for change. Matching clients with well-selected and tailored services significantly improves client outcomes. In a six-month study, researchers revealed that clients with case managers who helped coordinate treatment with medical care, employment needs, housing resources, and parenting needs (child care, skills training, etc.) had reduced substance use and lower incidence of mental and physical problems. This has been emphasized by the National Institute on Drug Abuse, which states that "matching treatment settings, interventions, and services to each individual's particular problems and needs is critical to his or her ultimate success in returning to productive functioning in the family, workplace, and society." Clearly, having a broad array of treatment options and ensuring that individuals are receiving optimal care are in the best interests of clients.

48. C: The idea that every individual must hit bottom in order to be ready to successfully complete treatment is a profound but still common misconception among the general population and even in the substance abuse treatment field. Research reveals that, even when individuals enter treatment for the "wrong reasons" (e.g., because of external pressures), their treatment outcomes are roughly equivalent to those entering for the "right reasons" (e.g., a true desire to change). External pressures such as negative personal, employment, or legal consequences may ultimately produce the internal motivations to change that are needed. In recognition of this, substance abuse treatment staff should generally deem a potential client's presence in the office as an indicator of a workable level of desire for treatment services.

49. C: Virtually every client will repeatedly waver in motivation and commitment at times. The best motivators to continue in treatment and to overcome addiction tend to be those things that clients have previously declared as being of importance to them. This can be honoring family relationships or wishes, avoiding legal problems, maintaining employment, maintaining health, or any number of other motivators. Regardless of the desired goal, client reminders about the personal motivators they already have tend to offer them the best long-term support. In contrast to this, playing to a client's fears tends to have an inuring and accommodating effect, losing its power over time. Threats also tend to polarize and drive clients away from their immediate commitments. Playing devil's advocate (i.e., "I knew you couldn't do it") typically only confirms a client's already deep fear of failure. Instead, positive reminders and encouragement induce a greater sense of motivation and more enduring commitment, especially if relapses occur.

50. A: In becoming ready to seek change and overcome past habits and addictions, clients typically go through five stages of change: (1) pre-contemplation, (2) contemplation, (3) action, (4) relapse, and (5) maintenance. By virtue of having entered treatment, the client is already at the action stage in the readiness process. Consequently, when client resistance to treatment is encountered, this resistance most likely indicates that the client has been pressured to move too quickly through the change process, leaving him or her little opportunity to respond with anything but resistance. Exploring the client's current rationale and determination to change can reveal where he or she is on the change continuum, enabling the counselor to better support the client along the way.

51. B: Research consistently reveals that the therapeutic alliance is of primary importance in clients achieving positive outcome. Among the many positive effects of the therapeutic alliance, treatment retention is one of the most significant. Consequently, achieving and maintaining a therapeutic alliance is crucial. The four key components of an effective therapeutic alliance are: (1) the client's capacity to purposefully work on the problem (providing a shared goal and common ground); (2) the affective (emotional) bond between the client and the therapist; (3) the therapist's possession of an empathic understanding of the client; and (4) agreement on the primary goals and between client and therapist. Counselors can enhance the therapeutic alliance by being empathic, nonjudgmental, and active listeners and by actively presenting the treatment process as a collaborative venture, rather than as one consisting of unilateral directives.

52. D: Researchers reveal that completion of any prescribed episode of treatment is a key to improved outcomes. The length of the episode is not the critical feature. Success produces meaningful momentum. In recognition of this, it is particularly important to retain clients in treatment programs, avoiding the high drop-out rates so common in the first few weeks of treatment. Steps to reduce drop-out include: preadmission interviews to ensure client readiness for treatment, the use of telephone and mail reminders of ongoing appointments and program activities, offering telephone orientations for timely program accommodation, and decreasing any delays in call-to-appointment scheduling. Finally, helping clients understand the underlying rationale behind lifestyle changes improves behavioral adherence and program retention.

53. D: Participation in twelve-step and other mutual-help programs is associated with better outcomes than participation in treatment programs alone. Indeed, clients who join a twelve-step program after treatment tend to do significantly better than those not so involved, researchers have found. Consequently, treatment providers should actually facilitate client integration into appropriate community-based mutual-help groups, including assisting clients to locate a group and a sponsor. This should involve more than referral. Counselors should help clients find the right group meeting milieu as well as helping them determine the optimal frequency of attendance. Clients who begin attending twelve-step groups frequently experience some minor negative side effects. These can be minimized by ensuring selection of an optimal group, along with adequate orientation and support.

54. A: The original twelve-step program, Alcoholics Anonymous (AA) had a significant religious orientation. Since that time, however, references to deity and religion in general have been moderated to better allow for individual values and beliefs. A group similar to AA but oriented toward those using narcotics is known as Narcotics Anonymous (NA). Some clients may also benefit from twelve-step support group alternatives such as Rational Recovery, Smart Recovery, or Women for Sobriety. Offering clients a variety of choices empowers them to make informed decisions. There are also twelve-step meetings designed to support the family members of loved ones suffering from substance abuse. These include: Al-Anon/Alateen and Nar-Anon. Other twelve-step groups exist for individuals coping with compulsive behaviors such as sex, gambling, spending, and eating. Helping clients and their family members to find and join appropriate mutual-help organizations can be an important part of treatment planning and continuing care.

55. B: Not all mental health conditions require long-term pharmacotherapy. In some cases, traditional pharmacotherapy may involve the use of dependency-producing medications that may not be appropriate for certain individuals. However, most individuals with co-occurring substance abuse and mental health disorders can receive well-chosen medications appropriate to their conditions. It is important not to rule out medication therapy out of hand as untreated mental health conditions can contribute greatly to substance abuse relapse. This can occur both in an effort to self-medicate and because untreated mental health problems can reduce otherwise adequate defenses against a return to substance abuse. Consequently, mutual-help groups have become more amenable to the use of necessary psychiatric medications.

56. A: Open-ended heterogeneous groups allow clinicians some flexibility in assigning new clients to ongoing groups. This permits immediate responsiveness to new and early client needs. However, those in these open-ended heterogeneous groups vary in their recognition and acceptance of their substance abuse. Thus, over time, it usually becomes necessary to move clients into progress- or issue-specific groups as unique needs and progress become apparent. Some clients make rapid progress from one stage to another, while others may need to return to an earlier treatment stage due to relapse or encountering other problems. In this way, the treatment process can be meaningfully individualized and tailored to the unique and changing needs of each client. Because of this, the group to which a given client was initially assigned is unlikely to remain unchanged throughout the treatment episode.

57. C: Treatment programs may choose to organize various homogeneous groups based on one or more demographic or therapeutically relevant issues for a unique subset of clients. Therapeutically relevant issues may include: those not fully ready for treatment (pre-contemplators and contemplators), similar drugs of choice, histories of sexual or physical abuse, single parenting, human immunodeficiency virus/acquired immunodeficiency syndrome (HIV/AIDS), and gender issues. Demographically unique groups include those organized solely for men or women, minority populations, or elderly persons. Other potential demographic groups include those based on socioeconomic status, legal issues (i.e., driving under the influence [DUI], probation, etc.), professions, or unemployment. Clients in these groups benefit from a shared perspective in working together. Other unique populations include clients with transient or enduring cognitive impairments, illiteracy, or second language needs. Programs should regularly assess their educational materials to ensure that they remain appropriate for each of the various groups involved.

58. D: Although these populations may benefit from same-drug-of-choice groups, there is no fundamental barrier to them being assigned to the same treatment group. However, abuse perpetrators and victims of abuse should never be assigned to the same group as the psychological impact and interactive dynamics would be profoundly detrimental, particularly for those with a history of significant victimization. Neighbors and relatives (including spouses) should also never share the same group as issues of disclosure, confidentiality, and other interactive inhibitions would likely become counterproductive over time. Clients with schizophrenia and those with antisocial disorders are not compatible group members as their psychological dynamics would inhibit or entirely thwart the treatment process. Indeed, clients with severe psychiatric disorders may require solely individual therapy. Clients that may need to be withdrawn from group include those who violate group standards and agreements, those who regularly drop out, and clients with significant impulse-control issues.

59. D: A common intensive outpatient treatment (IOT) program involves three hours of treatment on three days or evenings each week. Other programs meet five days or evenings per week. The schedule might involve back-to-back ninety-minute groups on two evenings. One provides opportunities for those in a similar recovery stage to share daily concerns, and the other might involve a psychoeducational topic. A third evening might include an hour-long skills training group, thirty minutes of individual counseling, and a ninety-minute family session. Group sessions are often ninety minutes, though the duration may vary according to need and group responsiveness. Psychoeducational sessions often consist of thirty-minute lectures followed by fifteen-minute question-and-answer periods. The shorter duration ensures client attention to instruction. Interactive group treatment periods are more engaging and thus more easily sustained for longer sessions. The expected duration of active treatment in IOT programs varies, but many span twelve to sixteen weeks. After active treatment concludes, clients step down to a maintenance phase that may extend for six months or more.

60. A: This size facilitates optimal treatment engagement without permitting individual neglect. Process-oriented groups may be more effective with only six to eight members as these middle- to late-phase groups focus more on daily issues, thoughts, emotions, behavior management, and new ways of relating to others. Psychoeducational groups can be larger as they primarily involve didactic content. Many group sessions are structured using a rule of thirds. The first third involves sharing current issues or experiences; the second third addresses a particular issue or skill; and, the final third is used to summarize learnings and assign an exercise. An alternative structure involves a problem-solving process: (1) an issue of concern is identified; (2) options and solutions are explored; (3) an optimal course is identified; and (4) an action plan is developed. This is followed by soliciting commitments from group members to attempt the solution and report the outcome. Finally, many recovery groups utilize opening and closing rituals that enhance commitments and group solidarity.

61. B: Buprenorphine is used in the treatment of physical opioid dependence as a newer alternative to Methadone. Disulfiram (Antabuse) and naltrexone (ReVia) are medications used in the treatment of alcohol dependence and most particularly in the avoidance of relapse. Disulfiram doses are effective for three days. Clients can receive the medication during group sessions, with additional doses sent home for use over the weekends. While early studies indicate that naltrexone does not reduce the frequency of relapses, it does appear to reduce the overall duration of relapse. It also helps to reduce the amount of alcohol consumed in a relapse episode. Of note, however, recent data suggest that naltrexone might not be effective for men with chronic and severe alcohol dependence. Another alcohol treatment medication, acamprosate (Campral), has been Food and Drug Administration (FDA)-approved for alcohol abstinence maintenance since 2004. Acamprosate decreases the amount, frequency, and duration of alcohol consumption during episodes of alcohol relapse. It also helps to reduce cravings, even if clients resume drinking.

62. A: Luminal is a barbiturate with no opioid management role. Opioid use disorder is very difficult to treat. Detoxification is insufficient, and relapse is common. Consequently, many clients may need maintenance on opioid substitutes that still enable them to function productively. These substitutes include methadone, buprenorphine (Subutex), and joint buprenorphine and naloxone preparations (sublingual Suboxone film and Zubsolv tablets). If crushed and injected, the naloxone precipitates opioid withdrawal but with no such effect sublingually. Frequently, clients are started on methadone, moved to Subutex, and then transitioned to Suboxone for maintenance. For those who desire eventual abstinence, gradual weaning from buprenorphine is much easier than from methadone. Another opioid substitute, levo-alpha acetyl methadol (LAAM), is still Food and Drug Administration (FDA)-approved, but the United States manufacturer ceased production in 2005. Both LAAM and methadone must be administered at limited-licensed clinics, while buprenorphine preparations can be prescribed at a doctor's office. This greatly reduces treatment burdens and has significantly benefitted clients.

63. D: Substance abuse disorders are commonly found in concert with other mental disorders. American Society of Addiction Medicine (ASAM) patient placement criteria recommend that individuals with no-, low-, and moderate-severity disorders be treated in standard intensive outpatient treatment programs (IOT)—provided they are capable of reasonably close coordination and collaboration with necessary mental health services. In this way, clients can still effectively receive psychological assessment and consultations, psychopharmacologic monitoring, and treatment of substance use disorders. In situations of high-severity psychiatric diagnoses, clients should be treated in programs with on-site dual mental health and substance use treatment programs and cross-trained staff. Low- to moderate-severity co-occurring mental disorders include anxiety and other stable mood disorders. High-severity disorders include mood disorders with psychotic features, schizophrenia, and borderline personality disorder.

64. C: Urine testing can identify a great number of substances. A breathalyzer can help identify alcohol, though its short biological life makes timely detection difficult. Monitoring of clients' substance use is essential to learn if the selected therapy is being successful. Objective tests, as opposed to self-reports, are typically needed to reliably and accurately monitor progress and increase the accuracy of self-reports. Monitoring helps identify the need for treatment plan modifications, assists families in reestablishing trust, aids clients in avoiding slips or lapses, and discourages substitution of another substance for their primary drug of choice. However, the purpose of testing is to limit substance use rather than to punish or produce shame and guilt. To this end, rewards for successful testing are preferred to punishment as this reinforces the desired behaviors rather focusing on failures. If positive tests must be reported outside the program, clients must be fully informed. In this way, trust can better be maintained, and the therapeutic alliance may be less negatively impacted.

65. C: There is no twelve-step group for hallucinogen abuse, probably because, other than PCP, hallucinogens do not produce a withdrawal syndrome. Participation in community twelve-step and other mutual-help groups is an important part of the treatment process. Help motivates clients through group and individual discussions regarding available programs. Clients should, in particular, understand that there are numerous program formats. For example, there are step meetings, open speaker meetings, and open and closed discussion meetings. Further, there are specialized groups such as those for women; the hearing impaired; for the lesbian, gay, bisexual, and transgender (LGBT) communities; for race and ethnicity groups; language-specific groups (e.g., Spanish); for agnostics; for youth; and for beginners. Finally, for those less comfortable with a twelve-step approach, there are alternatives such as: (1) self-management and recovery training; (2) secular organizations for sobriety; and (3) Save Our Selves—which all use a twelve-step-like process to promote individual empowerment, self-determination, and self-affirmation.

66. A: The copyrighted Alcohol Dependence Scale (ADS) is composed of twenty-five items that provide a quantitative measure of alcohol dependence, with a score of nine being highly predictive of a *Diagnostic and Statistical Manual of Mental Disorders* (DSM)-supported diagnosis. The five-minute test can be self-administered and covers: (1) alcohol withdrawal symptoms, (2) reduced control over drinking, (3) compulsive drinking awareness, (4) increased alcohol tolerance, and (5) key drink-seeking behaviors. The ADS has been widely used in research and in clinical settings, and numerous studies have determined that the instrument is both valid and reliable. The ADS offers excellent predictive value in establishing a DSM diagnosis. It also produces a measure of dependence severity that is needed in treatment planning, particularly regarding the intensity of treatment needed. ADS instructions for administration request responses regarding alcohol used during the immediate past twelve months. However, other selected intervals (e.g., six months, twelve months, or twenty-four months) may be applied following treatment. Use of the ADS has primarily been among clinical adult samples. However, studies have also used the ADS with adolescents.

67. C: The Composite International Diagnostic Interview (CIDI) covers both *Diagnostic and Statistical Manual of Mental Disorders* (DSM) and International Classification of Diseases (ICD-10) criteria for substance use disorders. It also addresses the consequences of substance use, the onset of some symptoms, including withdrawal, and various psychiatric diagnoses. Lifetime and twelve-month versions are available in multiple languages. Both interview and self-administered versions are available, requiring approximately seventy minutes to complete. While primarily designed as an epidemiological tool, the CIDI can readily be used for clinical tasks. Psychiatrically, the interview covers anxiety disorders, cognitive impairment, depressive disorders, eating disorders, mania, schizophrenia, somatoform disorders, and substance use disorders. Highly structured and complex, the interview can still be carried out reliably by trained non-clinicians. Computerized scoring yields DSM and International Classification of Diseases (ICD)-10 diagnoses. Reliability and validity have both been demonstrated in a variety of studies.

68. D: The Diagnostic Interview Schedule (DIS) provides diagnostic information about alcohol and other substance-use disorders as well as anxiety disorders, depression, eating disorders, schizophrenia, and antisocial personality disorder, among other psychiatric conditions. The instrument explores syndromes meeting *Diagnostic and Statistical Manual of Mental Disorders* (DSM) criteria over the past year along with information about the course of the disorders, functional impairments, and any perceived need for treatment, treatment utilization, and potential links between psychiatric and physical symptoms. It also establishes dates for more recent symptoms and risk factors. Primary concerns are: (1) it requires more than the ninety to one hundred twenty estimated minutes to administer (averaging two and one-half hours, per one study); and (2) it fails to consistently identify clients with depression or schizophrenia. However, the highly structured content and administration guidelines do allow trained non-clinicians to administer it accurately.

69. D: This instrument screens for major psychiatric disorders, based upon *Diagnostic and Statistical Manual of Mental Disorders* (DSM) and International Classification of Diseases (ICD)-10 criteria. It explores sixteen to twenty-four diagnostic concerns, depending upon the version being used. These include: depression, anxiety, mania, eating disorders, phobias, alcohol and drug abuse, antisocial personality, posttraumatic stress disorder (PTSD), and psychosis. The goal was to develop a structured interview tool shorter than most used in clinical trials and yet longer and more effective than the many brief screens being used—especially when used to track treatment outcomes. Carefully structured, it can be administered by non-clinician interviewers. For brevity, the focus is on current disorders. Using one or two screening questions, the diagnosis is promptly ruled out with negative answers. Inter-rater and test–retest reliability of the MINI was compared against the Composite International Diagnostic Interview (CIDI) and the Structured Clinical Interview for DSM patients (SCID). Kappa coefficient, sensitivity, and specificity were good or very good for all diagnoses, except for: (1) generalized anxiety disorder, (2) agoraphobia, and (3) bulimia. The MINI provided reliable diagnoses within a very brief time frame.

70. B: Antisocial personality disorder consists of a pervasive pattern of disregard for and violation of the rights of others, and a lack of empathy. Borderline personality disorder involves a pervasive pattern of instability in relationships, self-image, identity, behavior and affects, often leading to self-harm and impulsivity. The Psychiatric Research Interview for Substance and Mental Disorders (PRISM) instrument was designed to differentiate primary psychiatric disorders such as these from substance-related disorders. Specifically, it can be difficult to determine where psychiatric problems are either covered by or induced by a substance disorder and vice versa. Consequently, PRISM offers procedures for differentiating primary disorders, substance-induced disorders, and the effects of intoxication and withdrawal. Requiring between one and three hours to administer, PRISM can be particularly helpful in efforts to properly plan, refine, and focus needed treatment. Due to its complexity, interviewer training is required, and the scoring is computerized.

71. A: A genogram is a family relationship map that utilizes special symbols to trace consanguineous relationships, major events, and family dynamics over multiple generations. Genograms are often used to identify patterns of mental and physical illnesses, including issues of addiction. A genogram is dynamic as it is revised as often as new information is discovered. Genograms can also be created for a family of choice (nonbiological relationships, such as spouses, significant others, friends, etc.) from which similar patterns can be derived. Another mapping tool is the family social network map, which traces family and nonfamily communications, behaviors, emotional ties, social status, functions, and other connections. In substance abuse treatment, a social network assessment allows counselors to identify significant parties with key roles in a client's substance abuse trajectory. Because the concept of family has significantly expanded in modern times to include nonrelatives of considerable importance (a boyfriend or girlfriend or same-sex partner, friends, religious leaders, formal and informal social groups, etc.), social network mapping and analysis can be of considerable additional importance.

72. C: Community reinforcement training (CRT) improves the likelihood of entering and remaining in treatment. The community-reinforcement approach (CRA) supports abstinence by eliminating reinforcements for drinking and enhancing reinforcements for sobriety. An extension of this, the community reinforcement and family training (CRAFT) program teaches positive behavior rewards to encourage and support treatment. Families learn how to make sober activities more attractive and drug- or alcohol-using activities less inviting. They also learn to stop rescuing their loved one and instead allow the user to fully experience natural consequences. Clients entering treatment through confrontation are more likely to relapse than those encouraged into treatment. Family members also benefit by developing greater independence and learning skills that reduce symptoms of anger, anxiety and depression, even if their loved one does not accept treatment. CRAFT is culturally sensitive and works within a client's values and beliefs to develop a successful treatment plan. CRAFT research reveals that nearly seven of ten people using the program will successfully motivate a substance-using loved one to attend treatment.

73. D: Family education groups present information about substance abuse and its effects on the client and others, the issues of relapse and recovery, and family dynamics that may contribute to substance use. Families typically become more involved in treatment and more successful in wholesomely supporting the substance user. Groups typically meet two to three hours each week, often on weekends or evenings. Group size is normally between ten and forty individuals.

Facilitated by a counselor, common topics covered include: beginning stage (one to five weeks)—(1) commit to treatment, (2) the chronicity of a substance disorder, (3) ways to support abstinence, (4) identifying and eliminating behaviors that support substance use, and (5) other family resources (Al-Anon, Alateen, Nar-Anon, Families Anonymous, etc.); middle-stage work (six to twenty weeks) (1) relationship assessment, (2) eliminating enabling behaviors, (3) codependence, and (4) new communication methods; and advanced stage (twenty-on weeks and more) (1) development of a balanced lifestyle, (2) learning patience with recovery, and (3) evaluating and accepting limitations, adaptations, and changes over time.

74. B: A client who has experienced a lapse (sometimes called a slip) will: (1) have sustained abstinence for some time (a month or more; (2) return to treatment accountable and distressed because of the substance use; (3) be concerned regarding the potential consequences (legal issues, etc.); and (4) be open to talking about the episode and using it as an opportunity to better understand relapse triggers and pressures and to enhance relapse-prevention skills. Specifically, the client remains committed to recovery and is able to reassert control. When a relapse occurs: (1) the client avoids returning to treatment (and may return intoxicated); (2) there is a compulsive need to use; (3) the return to substance abuse is prolonged (days or more); and (4) the client is closed to intervention or learning. A relapse may well lead to treatment dropout and a renewed struggle by the client with his or her disease.

75. C: The entry of a client of some renown into a treatment group will typically have a number of disruptive dynamics. These may include: (1) increased risks to privacy and confidentiality (especially via the media); (2) feelings of privilege (regarding keeping program requirements); and (3) treatment milieu compromise (reductions in group cohesion, focus, trust, etc.). To mitigate problems, counselors must facilitate group assimilation as rapidly as possible by: (1) focusing on the private individual rather than his or her public persona; (2) clarifying treatment standards and requirements; and (3) obtaining a signed behavioral contract regarding confidentiality, privacy, and so on. The issue of a dual relationship may arise as a high-profile client may offer financial perks and personal appearances for the program or attempt to wield undue influence in other ways. Dual relationships are unethical, and no gifts or favors may be accepted beyond the published fee schedules. Only after a client has been out of treatment for an extended period (typically one year or longer) could program endorsements even be considered.

76. B: The potential client should not feel that it is required for him or her to seek treatment elsewhere, though he or she may choose to do so. Regardless, it is important for the counselor and the potential client to address any immediate concerns. This is usually handled best by way of a brief, private conversation between the two—perhaps in the privacy of the counselor's office. There, the existence of a prior social relationship can be acknowledged, and the potential client can be assured that the counselor will not involve him- or herself in the client's treatment in any way. Further, standards of confidentiality can also be explained, and the acquaintance can also be assured that he or she is fully in control of how to deal with this shared knowledge outside the treatment setting. To ensure the client's comfort and confidentiality as fully as possible, he or she must also discloses the acquaintance to supervising staff. In this way, the counselor can ensure that he or she will not ever be involved in the client's treatment in any way.

77. A: The Alcohol Abstinence Self-Efficacy Scale (AASE) is used to assess the level of a client's confidence in being able to abstain from alcohol use in twenty situations that include common drinking cues. The instrument uses forty items aggregated into four scales to determine a client's risk of relapse in the twenty situations. The four scales address: (1) situations of negative emotions that can readily trigger drinking (e.g., discouragement, depression, or frustration); (2) positive or exciting situations or feelings that may generate a desire to drink (e.g., vacations, holidays, celebrations, etc.); (3) circumstances of physical pain or distress that drinking might relieve (e.g., fatigue, headache, etc.); and (4) coping with cravings (e.g., testing one's willpower, just one drink, experimentation, etc.). The AASE can be administered via paper and pen and scored in about twenty minutes. There is no specialized training necessary to use it. Common uses include: (1) to evaluate clients at the time of program admission; (2) to evaluate and guide treatment; and (3) to create customized relapse prevention strategies; and so on.

78. B: The Alcohol Effects Questionnaire (AEQ) explores a client's expectations regarding both the positive and negative effects of drinking. Clients are asked to respond to forty exploratory statements about the effects of alcohol on them personally (rather than people in general). The AEQ instrument then provides scores in eight separate expectation categories: (1) generally positive feelings; (2) physical and social pleasure; (3) sexual enhancement; (4) increased feelings of power and aggression; (5) enhanced social expressiveness; (6) stress reduction and relaxation; (7) decreases in physical and cognitive capacity; and (8) careless unconcern (e.g., regarding actions, consequences, etc.). The AEQ can be administered and scored in about ten minutes, with no need for specialized training. Although typically used in research, the AEQ can also be used to assess a client's motivations for drinking and to explore alternative ways to more meaningfully achieve those effects. The AEQ has been particularly helpful in evaluating and redirecting the motivations of college students in their use of alcohol.

79. D: The Alcohol-Specific Role Play Test (ASRPT) uses powerful role-playing scripts to evaluate client responses to ten different high-risk relapse situations. The ASRPT guides clients through a series of taped prompts to which they act out their responses. Each response is videotaped for scoring purposes. In five of the situations, the client must role-play a response with another person. For example, the client is presented with a situation where a business contact insists that they complete a business deal over drinks at a bar. The client offers a videotaped response. The other five situations explore the client's responses to an internal conflict. For example, the client is presented with the scenario of a fully day's yard work, followed by a sudden desire to relax with a cold beer. The ASRPT can be administered in as little as twenty minutes and can accommodate either male or female role-play partners. Administration requires training, as does the scoring. It also requires the support of a videotape technician.

80. A: The Situational Confidence Questionnaire (SCQ) is a thirty-nine-item self-report questionnaire that explores self-efficacy in each of eight alcohol-related scenarios. Clients imagine themselves in each situation and then indicate on a six-point scale how confident they are in their ability to resist the urge to drink heavily in that situation. The responses produce a measurement of the development of a client's self-efficacy in specific drinking situations over the course of treatment. It is particularly useful identifying situations with the greatest risk of relapse, thus guiding relapse-prevention planning. Subscales help to identify pleasant or unpleasant emotions, physical discomfort, self-control testing, urges and temptations, conflict with others, social pressures to drink, and pleasant times with others. Each of these subscales can help the counselor and client to better identify what is driving the need to drink. The SCQ can be administered in about eight minutes. The minimal training required is available from a user's guide that can be obtained with the SCQ.

81. D: The higher power concept arises from twelve-step programs themselves. Cognitive-behavioral therapy (CBT) posits emotional and behavioral reactions are largely learned responses and that alternative responses can be learned. Thus, the CBT approach teaches clients how to recognize and limit relapse risks, behaviors to maintain abstinence, and techniques to improve self-efficacy while identifying cues or triggers (feelings, situations, and people) that may promote substance use. Triggers are either internal (e.g., stress responses, cravings, etc.) or external (e.g., people, places, or situations in which drugs were used). By analyzing triggers, adopting new recovery-oriented responses, and role-playing high-risk scenarios, clients develop the skills to resist substance use urges. CBT approaches also work well for other recovery challenges (e.g., relationships, mood management, etc.). CBT and twelve-step approaches complement each other well. Thus, many CBT-oriented programs encourage twelve-step program participation.

82. B: In point of fact, cognitive-behavioral therapy (CBT) was developed as an individual counseling approach. Its key strengths are: (1) its capacity to readily engage clients in therapeutic and experiential learning processes; (2) the ease with which it accommodates clients from very diverse experiences, beliefs, cultures, and other backgrounds, including those with great variation of their histories of alcohol and drug use (e.g., new single-substance users vs. long-term multi-substance abusers, etc.); and (3) it offers a clear understanding of relapse triggers and situations and readily enables alternative options. Its drawbacks include: (1) low suitability for clients with limited reading or cognitive skills (e.g., alternatives to written assignments may be necessary); (2) fairly extensive counselor training in CBT principles and techniques is necessary; and (3) clients must be motivated to change as relatively extensive homework is required.

83. C: Research reveals that clients provided with cognitive-behavioral therapy (CBT) more frequently reported substance-abuse avoidance strategies as long at one year following treatment, as compared with those clients who were taught contingency management techniques alone. Extensive randomized clinical trials have demonstrated that CBT relapse prevention treatment is unquestionably superior to only minimal treatment or no treatment at all in helping clients to avoid alcohol and drug use and maintain abstinence. Findings from the multiyear Project MATCH study found CBT to be as effective as both motivational enhancement therapy (MET) and twelve-step facilitation in reducing drinking and other alcohol-related problems. All three therapies resulted in positive improvements in participants' outcomes that persisted for as long as three years following treatment.

84. C: Motivational interviewing (MI) was developed by Miller and Rollnick. It utilizes techniques derived from numerous theoretical approaches that clarify the progressive stages of recovery. MI is designed to explore and lessen the uncertainty about accepting treatment by using an empathic, client-centered, yet directive counseling approach. This frequently involves building on clients' prior successes and the problem-solving strategies and solutions that supported those achievements. To be successful, MI requires a nonjudgmental, collaborative style that reveals the often disguised negative hazards and effects of substance abuse. Thus, the counselor serves as a coach or consultant, not as an expert or authority figure. Four basic MI principles are: (1) empathy—acknowledging and respecting the client's decisions yet noting the client's accountability for change; (2) discrepancy identification—contrasting current behavior with expressed ideals and goals; (3) resistance reduction—remaining neutral to client resistance, rather than confronting or correcting, to allow resistance to recede in the face of available information; (4) supporting self-efficacy—reflecting client strengths and encouraging a conviction that change can be achieved.

85. A: Motivational enhancement therapy (MET) is an adaptation of motivational interviewing (MI). MET uses MI strategies and techniques but also incorporates structured assessments and follow-up sessions. In these sessions, clients are provided feedback regarding substance use in multiple areas (e.g., societal norms and their level of use, physical and social consequences, relevant family history, readiness for change, and associated risk factors). This normative feedback is reviewed in a nonconfrontational manner by means of MI techniques (client-centered counseling to explore and resolve treatment ambivalence and achieve lasting changes). In this way, MET informs while also eliciting motivation to change by resolving ambivalence, evoking self-motivational statements, revealing a commitment to change, and rolling with resistance (e.g., responding neutrally to resistance rather than contradicting or correcting). MET is effective with all degrees of substance abuse, and court-mandated clients appear to benefit as much as self-referred clients. A four-session version of MET was found to be as effective as the other, more intensive interventions (i.e., cognitive-behavioral therapy [CBT] and twelve-step facilitation). Clients with anger issues achieved significantly more abstinent days.

86. B: The earliest Matrix Model was developed as a twelve-month version that included six months of intensive treatment with fifty-six individual or family counseling sessions. Counseling was provided three or four times each week, augmented with educational, family, relapse prevention, and social support groups. The first cocaine-specific treatment protocol was eventually revised to address alcohol and opioid use as well. Ultimately, cost constraints led to the development of a sixteen-week model that reduced individual sessions to three and focused more on group work. The individual program eventually expanded to include a twelve-week family and patient education group series and continuing care via an ongoing weekly social support group for continuing care. The program is rounded out with weekly drug testing (urinalysis) and encouragement to attend twelve-step meetings to supplement the intensive treatment and provide a continuing source of positive emotional and social support.

87. D: Stress and emotion management skills are integrated into the treatment process. Early recovery groups typically consist of new clients (first month of treatment) or those needing additional (or repeated) abstinence skills training. The primary goal is to educate clients about: (1) cognitive tools to reduce cravings; (2) classically conditioned biological cravings; (3) time management and scheduling skills; (4) essentials of secondary substance abstinence; and (5) needed community services linkages. Relapse prevention groups offer relapse education and supportive sharing. Topics focus on behavior change, altering cognitive and affective orientations, and establishing twelve-step program linkages. Social support groups consist of clients in the final month of treatment and focus on identifying drug-free activities and establishing and extending friendships with drug-free people. These groups are less structured, with content determined by group members' needs. Family education groups meet for twelve weeks to address topics such as: (1) addiction biology); (2) conditioned cues, extinction, and conditioned abstinence; (3) substance abuse health effects; and (4) addiction effects on the family.

88. D: A study reported significantly less cocaine use by the Matrix patients at eight months after treatment admission (monthly or more frequent cocaine use was four of thirty in the Matrix group, as compared to ten of twenty-three following inpatient treatment, and fourteen of thirty receiving no formal treatment). Another study revealed dramatic methamphetamine use reductions during treatment (eleven days of use in the past thirty at enrollment, reduced to about four days at treatment's end, decreasing to three days at twelve-month follow-up). A study of one hundred cocaine-dependent subjects randomly assigned to a six-month Matrix treatment condition versus other available community resources revealed fewer positive urine tests for Matrix subjects but not for community resource subjects at three and six-month follow-ups. Similarly, improved scores on the Addiction Severity Index (ASI) employment and family scales, and on a depression scale, were noted. Finally, in an eight-site study coordinated by the University of California, Los Angeles (UCLA), the program completion rate for Matrix participants was significantly higher (40.9 percent) than for treatment-as-usual participants (34.2 percent).

89. A: Some materials will require modification to work well for cognitively impaired clients, and retention can be a problem if the intense scheduling and structure is off-putting to clients. These are among the most problematic elements of the Matrix Model of treatment. Other problems can be more readily controlled or resolved. Among the many key positives of the Matrix Model are: (1) the model successfully integrates cognitive-behavioral therapy, routine urine testing, family involvement, psychosocial education, and twelve-step support—all of which are evidence-based steps to higher rates of abstinence over time; (2) the program is well structured, with a manual, predesigned handouts, complete educational components, and so on, allowing for successful staff application, and the model has been proven to be effective in numerous efficacy studies; and (3) the program is culturally responsive and sensitive to various other special-needs groups.

90. B: This theory posits that present and future behavior arises from the consequences (positive or negative) of past behavior. Substances used can provide both positively reinforcing effects (euphoria, etc.) and negative reinforcement (relief of psychic pain, avoidance of withdrawal, etc.). Desire for abstinence is typically an insufficient motivation, particularly at the outset. Therefore, other rewards that reinforce abstinence and a positive lifestyle change are usually required. Both community reinforcement (CR) and contingency management (CM) approaches motivate behavioral change and support abstinence by consistently rewarding desirable behaviors and ignoring or punishing other negative behaviors. CR uses relationships and other important life aspects—family and friends, job, hobbies, social events— to produce positive reinforcement. CM uses tangible rewards (events or objects) and punishments (fines, losses of privileges, etc.) to extinguish desires for substance abuse. Quitting one substance first may be a better goal than attempting to abstain from all substances. Starting with small changes can be a very effective strategy. Further, more frequent reinforcers (even if small), may be more effective than larger, more-distant rewards or punishments.

91. B: Co-occurring disorders require intensive primary treatment that is individualized according to diagnosis, phase of treatment, level of functioning, and level of care. Other factors include disorder acuteness, severity, medical safety, motivation, and availability of recovery support. Osher and Kofoed developed a staged-approach model with four overlapping stages geared to the client's current motivation and recovery level while also addressing varying degrees of severity and disability. The four stages are: (1) engagement, (2) persuasion, (3) active treatment, and (4) relapse prevention. The model consists of low-intensity but highly structured treatment, detoxification, toxicology screening, family involvement, and mutual-help group support. It also has a case management component to link clients with outside resources. Treatment of clients with substance use and high-severity psychiatric disorders (e.g., schizophrenia or bipolar disorder) differs markedly from treatment for anxiety or mood disorders. The more successful approaches integrate psychiatric and substance abuse treatments to meet the needs of the client. Approaches such as cognitive-behavioral therapy address both disorders, as does relaxation training, stress management, and skills training.

92. D: These clients are often unable to cope with stressful interpersonal experiences. Where depression and anxiety are predominant symptoms, they easily become overwhelmed. Where major psychiatric symptoms exist, internal stimuli (e.g., hallucinations, delusions, etc.) may surface and overwhelm them. Dual-diagnosis clients respond best when the counselor is both empathic and firm. The empathic approach reduces stress, and firm expressions help set boundaries and structure the experience. Further, feedback that addresses conflicting thoughts or problem behavior should be offered in a very factual and straightforward way. If delivered thoughtfully, the feedback can be both confrontive (compelling) and supportive. Approaches such as these are essential to a positive therapeutic alliance. Dual-diagnosed clients are prone to demoralization and despair because they experience especially slow improvement due to complex coping with two (or more) disorders. Instilling hope is an essential clinician task. Suggestions include: (1) show acceptance and understanding; (2) assist the client to express genuine concerns; (3) empower the client to help him- or herself; and (4) listen well and express empathy often.

93. D: Group treatment with clients with co-occurring disorders is well accepted and widely used. Group therapy has succeeded in increasing abstinence rates and in decreasing the need for hospitalization. However, group processes and approaches may require modification to meet the needs of dual-diagnosed clients. Augmenting group processes with individual counseling may be particularly helpful. The capacity to participate in counseling depends upon a client's level of functioning, symptom stability, medication compliance and responses, and potential cycles in mental status. Some dual-diagnosed clients may be unable to cope with the emotional intensity of group interactions; others may find it difficult to focus enough to meaningfully participate. Clients with serious mental illnesses such as schizophrenia or paranoid personality may need to be gradually incorporated into a group at their own pace. Suggestions for group work with co-occurring disorders include: (1) keep communications brief, simple, concrete, and repetitive as needed; (2) focus on accomplishments rather than failures, and resolve negative behaviors quickly and positively; (3) be responsive and sensitive to the client's needs, use shorter sessions and smaller groups, and use gentle, focused directional techniques.

94. A: Many dual-diagnosed clients fare best in mutual-help groups specifically geared to those with co-occurring disorders. As all group members have co-occurring disorders, these so called double-trouble groups do a better job of accommodating psychiatric symptoms and supporting the use of necessary psychotropic medications. Double-trouble groups are not structured to offer formal counseling but instead allow members to support one another in achieving and maintaining recovery and holding each other accountable. Some of the more widely recognized groups include: (1) Double Trouble in Recovery; (2) Dual Disorders Anonymous; (3) Dual Recovery Anonymous; and (4) Dual Diagnosis Anonymous. Early research suggests that traditional twelve-step groups may be beneficial for clients with mild-to-moderate co-occurring psychiatric disorders. However, in cases of severe mental disorders, many clients may have difficulty attending traditional twelve-step groups. Some clients may choose to participate in both dual disorder and traditional mutual-help groups. Where they do, studies reveal that most Alcoholics Anonymous (AA) members respond positively, and as many 93 percent support the individual's adherence to his or her psychotropic medication regimen.

95. D: Medication management groups may offer a great many opportunities and services. However, they are primarily created to help clients learn about medications they take, the intended effects and possible side effects, how to use the medications safely, and how to better understand the need for compliance. Other kinds of groups that may be created in substance abuse treatment programs include: (1) onsite support groups that provide a forum for exploring problems, enhancing and maintaining treatment progress, and practicing new skills; (2) psychoeducational groups that are designed increase clients' awareness of both substance abuse and any psychological problems in a supportive, safe, and information-rich environment; (3) psychiatric disorders groups that address co-occurring disorder topics such as signs and symptoms of mental disorders, the proper and necessary use of medications, and the potential effects of substances of abuse on mental disorders and the treatment process; and (4) social skills training groups that offer training in managing abstinence-averse social situations by teaching clients to seek support, refine refusal skills, and create ways to ensure compliance with prescribed treatment medications.

96. D: Studies indicate that the prevalence rates for major depression may vary from 2 to 19 percent across different countries. Studies indicate less heritability for major depression than for conditions such as schizophrenia and bipolar disorder. Instead, the evidence points to cultural factors, such as poverty, violence, and other stressful social factors primarily contributing to the onset of major depression. By contrast, studies in Europe, North America, and parts of Asia reveal that the prevalence of schizophrenia is similar worldwide (approximately 1 percent of a population), as is the lifetime prevalence of panic disorder (0.4–2.9 percent) and bipolar disorder (0.3–1.5 percent). The consistency in prevalence and symptoms of these disorders, coupled with the results of numerous family and molecular genetic studies, reveals a high heritability. In other words, it appears that culture and social factors are not generally causative of these disorders.

97. A: They ways that clients describe (or present) their symptoms may vary substantially across cultures. Asian clients, for example, are more likely to report somatic (physical) symptoms while omitting those of an emotional nature. Yet, when questioned specifically about emotional symptoms, these same clients will acknowledge them. Thus, clients from differing cultures may choose to selectively identify or omit symptoms in culturally acceptable ways. Cultures may also ascribe different meanings to an illness. These are typically derived from deep-seated attitudes and beliefs about whether an illness is real or imagined, arising from the body or the mind (or both), whether it may elicit sympathy, the potential degree of stigma attending it, potential causal factors, and a sense of the kind of person that might contract or succumb to it. These meanings ultimately determine whether or not a client feels motivated to seek treatment, ways they may cope with their symptoms, whether or not their family and community will be supportive, and from whom they seek help (doctor, counselor, religious leader or traditional healer, etc.).

98. B: Suicide rates are lowest for African American women and highest for American Indian and Alaskan Native males. While the exact etiology for the wide divergence in rates is unknown, it is expected that cultural and social contexts in each subgroup will be explanatory. Mental illness arises from a complex interaction between cultural, social, psychological, and biological factors. Overall, research reveals that approximately 20 percent of the U.S. population (children and adults) will have a diagnosable mental health disorder at any given time. Insufficient studies have been conducted to determine prevalence by ethnic or other sociocultural factors. Early studies do, however, support sociocultural differences. For example, following treatment for schizophrenia, people who returned to families where criticism, hostility, or intensely expressed emotions had higher relapse rates than those whose family members expressed less negative emotion. Further, a study comparing Mexican American and white families found that, among Mexican American families, interaction patterns that were distant or lacking warmth predicted relapse better than interactions featuring criticism.

99. B: Racial and ethnic minorities are less inclined to seek treatment from mental health specialists. They turn more often to primary care medical providers. Other more frequently selected sources of support include clergy, traditional healers, family, and friends. African Americans often rely on ministers, who may carry out a variety of mental health roles (e.g., counselor, diagnostician, and referral provider). When they do utilize mental health services, many African Americans prefer counselors of the same race or ethnicity. African Americans often prefer counseling over drug therapy, citing concerns of addiction, side effects, and effectiveness. In avoiding mental health professionals, 50 percent of African Americans cited a fear of treatment and hospitalization, as compared to 20 percent of whites with similar concerns. Mistrust arises from both historical and present-day struggles with racism and discrimination, including perceptions of mistreatment by medical and mental health professionals. A recent survey revealed that 15 percent of Latinos and 12 percent of African Americans felt a doctor or health provider had judged them unfairly or treated them with disrespect because of their race or ethnic background, as compared with 1 percent of whites expressing such feelings.

100. A: The U.S. surgeon general portrayed stigma as the most formidable obstacle to mental illness and health. Stigma consists of negative beliefs and attitudes that cause others to avoid, discriminate, fear, or reject individuals with mental illness. To escape the shame and embarrassment of stigma, those with mental problems may conceal symptoms and avoid treatment. This limits their access to resources and opportunities and leads to hopelessness, poor self-esteem, and isolation. Many Asian cultures feel that mental illness reflects poorly on one's family lineage, ultimately diminishing marriage and economic prospects for other members of the family in the process. A Los Angeles study revealed that only 12 percent of Asians would share fears of mental health problems with a friend or relative (compared with 25 percent of whites). And, only 4 percent would seek help from a mental health specialist (compared with 26 percent of whites). And only 3 percent would seek help from a physician (versus 13 percent of whites). Clearly, the cultural sense of stigma has far-reaching effects.

101. A: Because many research instruments do not ask about sexual orientation, very little reliable information is available on substance abuse among lesbian, gay, or bisexual (LGB) individuals. However, research does indicate that lesbian, gay, bisexual, and transsexual (LGBT) individuals use alcohol and drugs more often than the general population. They are also more likely than the general population to persist in drinking heavily into later life and less likely to stop using drugs. On average, members of the LGBT community also use more kinds of drugs, including those that more profoundly impair judgment, such as amyl nitrite (poppers), Ecstasy, ketamine (Special K), and gamma hydroxybutyrate. These drugs are frequently used at parties and raves, during and after which increased risky sexual behavior may lead to human immunodeficiency virus/acquired immunodeficiency syndrome (HIV/AIDS) or hepatitis infections. Cultural groups differ in how they view their LGBT members. In Hispanic culture, matters of sexual orientation tend not to be discussed openly. LGB members of minority groups often find themselves targets of discrimination within their minority culture and of racism in the general culture.

102. D: The culture brokering approach was conceived to mediate the difficult gap between the needs of foreign-born people and the U.S. health care system. This model can also help clients with disabilities and impairments. Almost one-sixth of all U.S. citizens have some functional disability. Of these, more than 30 percent live below the poverty line, and most expend considerable financial resources on their disability-related needs. The combination of depression, frequent pain, employment difficulties, and functional limitations leaves the cognitively and physically disabled vulnerable to substance abuse. Yet, research reveals, they are less likely to receive effective treatment than those without any disability. Further, many disabled (and other) individuals struggling with addiction have unidentified learning disabilities that can impair successful treatment. Even individuals with the same disability may differ in their functional capabilities and limits. Consequently, treatment providers must carefully assess these clients and tailor treatments to meet their unique needs.

103. A: The rate of alcohol use among adults over the age twenty-five is lower in rural areas than that found in metropolitan areas. However, youth between the ages of twelve and seventeen have rates of heavy alcohol use that are almost double those in metropolitan areas. Further, rates of alcohol use and alcoholism among women in rural areas are higher than rates among women in metropolitan areas. Even so, at least one study reveals that individuals living in urban settings were treated for substance abuse more than twice as often as those living in a rural setting. It was concluded that the stigma of substance abuse treatment and the availability of treatment combined to substantially limit the treatment rate. Given that 20 percent of the U.S. population lives outside of metropolitan areas, understanding the unique needs of rural populations is important.

104. B: In other words, 75 percent will not receive proper treatment. Although the homeless receive detox services more than three times as often as people who are not homeless (45 percent vs. 14 percent), this is likely due to unexpected hospitalizations, psychiatric facility transitioning, and vagrancy and drug possession arrests that result in an involuntary detox and loose medical supervision. Of the approximately six hundred thousand homeless at any given time, about 41 percent are white, 40 percent are African-American, 11 percent are Hispanic, and 8 percent are Native American—disproportionate minority representation. The homeless may be: (1) transient—temporarily with others and at high risk of suddenly being on the street; (2) recently displaced—due to eviction or other financial problems (potentially due to substance abuse; or (3) chronically homeless—often with severe substance use and mental disorders, they are difficult to draw into treatment and are in need of creative outreach and programming initiatives.

105. C: Alcohol is the primary substance of abuse for 50 percent of the homeless admitted to treatment, with 18 percent abusing opioids (pain meds, heroin, etc.) and 17 percent abusing crack cocaine. Nearly one-quarter of the homeless (23 percent) have co-occurring disorders, while 20 percent of those not homeless also suffer with a co-occurring disorder. Recommendations for retaining homeless clients in treatment include: (1) meet their survival needs (food, clothing, warmth, and safe shelter) in addition to treatment and extensive continuing care; (2) optimally, early intensive treatment (clients attending 4.1 days per week have better outcomes than those attending fewer days); and (3) case management, which is needed to: (1) arrange safe and drug-free housing (which powerfully influences recovery, especially if housing is contingent on abstinence), (2) coordinate psychiatric and medical care, and (3) locate vocational training or education to help individuals become self-sufficient. The Alcohol Severity Index, the Alcohol Dependence Scale, and the personal history form have all been deemed valid and reliable screening tools for this population, especially when interviewed in a protected setting, with factual questions based on a recent time period.

106. A: This approach endeavors to evaluate and determine clients' needs in order to help them access specific resources. Client contacts are minimal, and planning is brief, as the goal is prompt and accurate referral without establishing an intensive, long-term relationship. Consequently, there is little to no monitoring or proactive advocacy. Because of this, the Brokerage or Generalist model is not always ideal, yet the limited relationship allows for cost-effective rendering of services to a greater number of clients. This approach works best when treatment and social services are well integrated, thus limiting the need for advocacy and monitoring. The optimal client is not economically deprived, has otherwise adequate resources, and is not in late-stage addiction. Smaller agencies that offer narrowly defined services may benefit most from this model. In some situations, case managers may also serve as educators, offering sessions on substance abuse and related high-risk behaviors.

107. C: Developed as a mental health treatment model, key elements of PACT include: (1) meeting clients in homes and other natural settings; (2) addressing practical daily problems; (3) advocating assertively; (4) limiting caseloads to ensure effectiveness; (5) regular client–case manager contacts; (6) caseloads shared by a team; and (7) long-term client services. First adapted for use with chronic alcoholics, the model deviated from a typical approach in two ways: (1) case managers used an enforced contact strategy to meet clients at home and in the field, and (2) the focus was on alleviating suffering rather than requiring a pledge of total abstinence. An adaptation of PACT, the Assertive Community Treatment (ACT) model is used to provide direct counseling and the skills needed to succeed in a community setting. Case managers provide crisis intervention, family consultation, and group facilitation—teaching about human immunodeficiency virus/acquired immunodeficiency syndrome (HIV/AIDS), work skills, and relapse prevention. As opposed to PACT, the ACT model is time limited, and extended abstinence and treatment completion is expected. ACT can be implemented alone or in concert with a therapeutic community.

108. D: This approach was developed to assist those with persistent mental illness to transition from institutional care to independent living. Two foundational principles are: (1) assisting clients in assuming direct control over their own search for resources (e.g., transportation, housing, employment, etc.), and (2) drawing upon clients' strengths in the acquisition of resources. This model focuses on informal helping networks (rather than institutional networks), supported through the client–case manager relationship. To achieve goals, the case manager maintains an active client outreach. The strengths case management perspective is used with substance abusers for three reasons: (1) case management facilitates client responsibility in finding and accessing resources needed for an enduring recovery; (2) the advocacy component counters the belief that substance abusers are morally deficient or in denial and thus unworthy of support; and (3) the emphasis on client strengths, assets, and abilities counterbalances treatment models that emphasize pathology and disease. Advocacy and client-driven goal planning can at times cause stress between the case manager and other members of a treatment team, but the approach clearly leads to improved client outcomes.

109. B: The case management clinical or rehabilitation approaches integrate clinical therapy and resource activities together. Both needs are met by the case manager rather than separate providers. Researchers have posited that it is not feasible or functional to divide these two activities for an extended time. To this end, the Clinical or Rehabilitation model merges these two activities by training case managers to see beyond solely environmental issues to other client-focused needs. To this end, the case manager is positioned to provide psychotherapeutic services, offer family therapy, and teach essential skills in a variety of areas, including relapse prevention, and so on. Beyond the usual repertoire of case management functions (assessment, planning, linkage, monitoring, and advocacy [per the Joint Commission on Accreditation of Healthcare Organizations] or assessing, arranging, coordinating, monitoring, evaluating, and advocacy [per the National Association of Social Workers]), the case manager should also address issues of transference, countertransference, client internalizations of observations, theories of ego functioning, and so on. In this way the client's needs can be met in a more holistic and integrated fashion, which should lead to enhanced outcomes.

110. D: The case manager's advocacy role is to identify and secure a client's best interests. This involves a dual responsibility—advocating for a client's genuine needs to be met and holding clients accountable when necessary. There are times when an institution is overlooking its responsibilities or even failing to meet those duties ascribed to it by contract, law, or legislative policy, and so on. In such situations, the case manager must advocate for the services that should be provided to the client, even if it requires confronting the institution or agency. In like manner, there are times when a client is failing to meet responsibilities and must be held accountable. At such times, it may be necessary for the case manager to advocate for sanctions, reporting, or other exclusions in order to ensure the client recognizes the neglected responsibilities, compliance, or performances that are required.

111. C: Both case management and client advocacy are subsets of service coordination, and resource linkage is one of the direct activities involved in each of these endeavors. Service coordination provides an action framework by which a client is enabled to achieve the specific goals identified in a treatment plan. It requires collaborative efforts not only between a case manager or counselor and a client but also with significant others as well as liaison activities with available agencies, service providers, managed care systems, and other community resources. Fundamental to service coordination is ongoing evaluation of client needs and treatment progress as well as resource referrals and advocacy as needed. The coordination and integration of treatment activities shared among various providers is a central feature of service coordination.

112. A: This individual is the one most comprehensively responsible to evaluate, track, and coordinate the broad array of resources and services that a client is receiving in the treatment process. A service coordinator may assume some of these roles but is less involved in the clinical assessment and evaluation processes. A counselor or therapist may be very involved in clinical evaluations and assessments but would not typically be as involved in service coordination. Finally, an administrator looks after the management of a program or agency and thus would not typically be involved in frontline client evaluations and assessments or referrals and service coordination. Case management, however, addresses: assessment and evaluation (client capacity, progress and readiness, as well as agency, program, and resource availability and effectiveness), service coordination, referrals and referral network management, monitoring, tracking, problem solving, advocating, negotiating, offering liaison services, and arranging and carrying out the resource needs of a treatment plan.

113. B: The use of a Qualified Service Organization Agreement (QSOA) is only indicated when an outside official or agency is providing services directly to a treatment program or agency itself. Any disclosure under the auspices of a QSOA is strictly limited to that information necessary for the service provider to ensure that the program or agency is able to function effectively. In turn, the QSOA stipulates that the service provider (i.e., the official or the contracted agency) is legally bound to resist any judicial proceedings seeking client information outside federal confidentiality standards and to maintain these same confidentiality standards in managing, processing, storing, and releasing any client information. In this way, the service provider is properly informed of relevant information to offer advice, consultations, and administrative insights necessary for the program or agency to efficiently and effectively carry out its necessary functions.

114. D: The Screening, Brief Intervention, and Referral to Treatment (SBIRT) public health approach is designed for use in hospital emergency departments, trauma centers, primary care clinics, and other health care settings. The goal is to identify diagnosable substance abuse disorders as well as those at-risk for developing a disorder before serious consequences develop. Each key component has a specific function toward this end: (1) screening—identifying and rapidly assessing substance use severity and determining the appropriate treatment level needed; (2) brief intervention—enhancing clients' awareness and insights regarding substance abuse consequences as well as motivating the client toward behavioral change; (3) referral to treatment—linking clients to specialized substance abuse treatment options as assessment indicates is needed and appropriate.

115. B: The ability to work with genuine compassion for clients is the first essential feature of successful counseling, provided appropriate boundaries are also maintained. Skills, knowledge, and information specific to the client's situation and needs are essential but are substantially ineffective if not managed with compassion and care. The renowned psychologist Carl Rogers taught that every individual has a positive, trustworthy center if this psychological core can be accessed. Connecting with this center taps into an individual's resourcefulness and capability for self-understanding and positive self-direction. To this end, he promoted three keys: (1) congruence (genuineness); (2) unconditional positive regard (caring concern and compassion); and (3) accurate, empathetic understanding (the ability to meaningfully assume the client's subjective perspective). Using these tools, clients can be reached and motivated toward positive change.

116. C: The pioneering University of California, Los Angeles (UCLA) nonverbal communication researcher Albert Mehrabian has revealed that approximately 50 percent of all communication is exchanged nonverbally in the form of body language. According to Mehrabian, there are three fundamental elements in face-to-face communication: (1) the actual words used; (2) the tone of voice used; and (3) nonverbal behaviors (e.g. facial expression, body posture, gestures, etc.). If the nonverbal elements are incongruent, the behavior and tonality tend to be seen as more genuine than any words expressed. Given the importance of genuine compassion and empathy in the therapeutic process, body language is particularly important. To optimize nonverbal communication, the counselor should be seated two to four feet from the client, with no intervening barrier (e.g., a desk), leaning forward, legs and arms uncrossed, hands open, nodding to communications expressed, and making direct eye contact (if cultural permits it). The client's body movements (including micro-movements, such as nostril flaring or quivering chin) should be noted and responded to appropriately.

117. A: Individuals with a history of substance abuse often come out of families, relationships, and environments with few if any boundaries or rules. Further, due to long-standing issues of shame and embarrassment over substance abuse, clients are often overly sensitive to feelings of critique and failure. Consequently, it is particularly important for clients to become aware of the rules, regulations, and boundaries of treatment program participation in advance. In this way, clients need not be surprised when redirected to existing boundaries and standards of conduct. In turn, this consistency creates an environment that feels more stable, predictable, and safe from the clients' perspective, which is important as they work to muster and maintain the motivation to make important changes in their lives. The program's informed consent process also leads naturally into identifying and establishing the early treatment goals needed to motivate, shape, and monitor clients' success.

118. C: The Substance Abuse and Mental Health Services Administration (SAMHSA) maintains the National Registry of Evidence-Based Programs and Practices (NREPP), which is a database of evidence-supported approaches to substance abuse counseling. The goal is to make available those theories, strategies, programs, and practices that have been proven effective in the treatment of substance abuse disorders. The database includes approaches such as twelve-step facilitation therapy, cognitive-behavioral therapy (CBT), and motivational interviewing (MI), among others. The database offers evaluations, recommendations, and suggestions to optimize the effectiveness of the various programs reviewed. The database is readily accessible via the Internet, and counselors should become familiar with the various programs, techniques, theories, and approaches offered to ensure optimal practices and program outcome effectiveness.

119. B: There are many things that offer indication of readiness for change. Clients having hit bottom and families that have reached a breaking point are often poised for change. A skilled counselor can sometimes create a false bottom by breaking through denial using a pointed but caring presentation of reality in such a way as to motivate change. Engaging the family in the recovery process is often as important as engaging the client in recovery. Families have to deal with their own emotional pain and shame and learn how to make choices from the perspective of whether or not each choice will help or hinder the recovery of their loved one. Learning to avoid enabling patterns is also crucial, along with family referrals to support groups and literature sources that will ensure understanding and enduring commitment to the recovery process.

120. C: A common rule of thumb in the field of substance abuse treatment is that the age at which significant substance abuse began is the point at which personal progress through normal developmental stages was arrested or missed altogether. Thus, people who began heavy drug use in their mid-teens will often have failed to master the developmental stages from that point forward until they returned to sobriety. Thus, teen issues of self-esteem, self-image, balanced relationships with the opposite sex, responding to authority, impulse control, and so on, will likely still need to be mastered. One role of the counselor will be to identify, inventory, and produce a learning plan to belatedly secure these important developmental learning tasks. To more fully structure the process of growth, clients will need to learn to adhere to a healthy living schedule—including timely morning wake-up, personal hygiene and living space cleanup, set meal times, work, group meetings, personal exercise and meditation, and wholesome bedtimes.

121. A: Issues of control over others are not prominent in reasons to begin or continue using drugs. Patterns of intrafamilial interaction that are common in families with substance abuse include: (1) negativity—criticism, complaints, and expressions of displeasure dominate, which may then reinforce the need for substance abuse; (2) misdirected anger—resentment over an emotionally deprived home ruled by fear encourages drug use to cope; (3) boundary inconsistency—unpredictable rules, inconsistent responses, and erratic boundaries lead to family member stress (especially among children), misbehavior, and a greater likelihood of substance abuse; (4) self-medication—coping with anxiety, depression, or intrusive thoughts can lead to substance abuse; (5) unrealistic expectations—leads family members to opt out through drug use; (6) denial—excusing or denying substance abuse allows its perpetuation. Where present, a complete restructuring of the family system, with education and interventions, is needed to abate any of these highly problematic issues.

122. D: Programmed confrontation is a method used to mobilize a substance user (typically a husband) to accept treatment. It is carried out by a family member (typically a wife). To effectively engage programmed confrontation, the family member receives training in Unilateral Family Therapy (UFT). The training is conducted over a period of months, covering important issues such as personal coping (with the addict's abuse), helping him or her cut back on substance use, and ways to encourage treatment acceptance. By the fifth month, the addict is typically prepared. UFT was influenced by the community reinforcement approach (CRA), and the Johnson Intervention. The Johnson Intervention utilizes family mobilization, coaching, and rehearsing to motivate a potential client into treatment—usually using an element of surprise. The model focuses on the addict's positive traits and the negative changes that result from addiction. Specific examples of behavior issues are presented in a loving, caring manner to break through the addict's denial and encourage treatment. The UFT success rate is 37 percent entering treatment, compared to 11 percent where no UFT techniques were involved.

123. C: Community reinforcement training (CRT) is an approach used by families to hasten a user into treatment. The initial step involves seeing users' loved ones who call for help on a same-day basis. At this first contact, they are enrolled in a training program to learn the steps needed to produce motivation and change. The program begins by teaching the family members how to produce a safety plan for themselves if they are in any way at risk of physical abuse. Then they are taught how to encourage abstinence, followed by ways to encourage treatment seeking. Finally, when the addict reaches a crisis point, the program is structured to bring him or her into treatment virtually immediately, regardless of the time of day or night. In one study, this nonconfrontational and expedited approach resulted in 86 percent of users entering treatment, while none of those using a traditional approach were successfully engaged.

124. C: The ARISE method uses a three-level approach to motivate an addict to enter treatment. Level 1 (The First Call) begins with a telephone consultation, followed by a first meeting of an intervention network (IN). The IN consists of immediately involved significant others (spouse, family, and close friends) who then meet with the addict to encourage treatment. Faced with the collective encouragement of the IN, approximately 56 percent of addicts will then enter treatment. Level 2 (Strength in Numbers) expands the IN to include more family, friends, potentially even employers, and a therapist, citing specific examples of concerns and the need for treatment. The IN acts in concert to avoid no-win one-on-one contacts. Within two to five meetings 80 percent will enter treatment. Level 3 (Formal Intervention) is more confrontational, as significant consequences of avoiding treatment are spelled out (all enabling behaviors to stop with more serious consequences to follow). Another 3 percent (i.e., 83 percent in total) will then accept treatment, and 61 percent of all will still be sober by the end of the first year.

125. D: This education can help the family to collaborate in the changes needed for the client to achieve and sustain sobriety throughout his or her life. Other benefits of drawing the family in include: (1) increase the client's motivation to change; (2) alter family patterns that may be obstacles to recovery; (3) help the family anticipate needs and issues through the various recovery stages; (4) teach relapse warning signs they can identify; (5) teach a family perspective on the causes and effects of substance abuse; (6) coopting family strengths on behalf of the client; and (7) help the family to find long-term support. In this way, support is optimized, client progress is maximized, family welfare is preserved, and outcomes are improved.

126. C: Men are much less likely to participate in the treatment of their female partners. Common obstacles to family involvement include: (1) resistance from the addict; (2) domestic violence issues; (3) family secrets that might come out; and (4) family resource burdens. Approaches to overcome resistance to family involvement include: (1) request family participation in intake (encouraging this with the client as well), citing policy, history intake needs, help for the client, and family support as reasons; (2) ask the client to collaborate in planning the family engagement; (3) send family a written invitation; (4) provide incentives (refreshments, coupons, etc.); (5) offer food (picnics, dinners, etc.); (6) program resources (babysitting, children's toys, flexible hours, etc.); (6) welcome environment (clean, cheerful, etc.); (7) ice-breaking activities (games, role-play, activities, etc.); (8) use community reinforcement training (CRT) to teach that the family is not to blame and that substance abuse isn't a moral flaw in addition to teaching them how to meet personal and family needs, how to support the client, and so on, to help increase understanding and make them feel more welcome and positive.

127. A: Bowen family systems theory views the family as an integrated emotional unit, best described and understood via a systems perspective when attempting to describe the complex interactions that arise in the unit. Family members are intensely emotionally connected and profoundly influence the feelings, thoughts, and actions of each other. They seek attention, support, and approval from each other and respond to one another's distress, needs, and expectations. Changes in the functioning of any one member will be followed by reciprocal changes in the others. From this perspective, family genograms, disruption history (e.g., immigration, holocaust, etc.), individual questioning, and orienting the members toward facts (versus reactions) can help improve family understandings and function. Coaching individuals into changes in interaction patterns can reduce triangulation and overall family anxiety.

128. B: Network therapy builds an extended collection of involved persons (social workers, school counselors, legal representatives, therapists, etc.) to meet, motivate, and reinforce changes and progress in the family. Extensive interviews help determine family needs and appropriate referrals to resources such as support groups, counseling, and so on, to help break the cycle of addiction. Other therapeutic options include: (1) Multidimensional family therapy uses support groups, interviews, and therapeutic interactions to discover issues, map out responses, and contract with involved family members to address, curtail, or resolve key family issues. New family skills, such as better communication and conflict resolution, relapse prevention, and coping strategies for any psychiatric disorders in the family, are all needed for enhanced family functioning. (2) Cognitive-behavioral family therapy uses factual constructs, improved communication and negotiation skills, contingency contracting, and better problem definitions to produce enhanced family functioning. (3) Structural or strategic systems therapy restructures roles, realigns subsystems and boundaries, and reestablishes more extended intergenerational boundaries to improve family function and cohesion.

129. D: This form of brief therapy focuses on helping clients to identify solutions to vexing problems. Asking clients to recall a time when the problem was not present or so severe, and then asking what they or others had done differently, can help in identifying potential solutions. Further, asking about exceptions to the problem (when it could have occurred but didn't) can also be helpful. Using the miracle question involves asking this: "If a miracle occurred and the problem went away, what would be the first sign (and then what signs would follow)?" Scaling questions allow clients to scale a problem from 0 (worst) to 10 (resolved) and then to discuss why they selected that number to find clarity (comparing couples or family answers can also help). Coping questions ask "How have you managed to carry on to this point?" to find strengths. Using consultation breaks at the half-session mark and pondering the answers, followed by compliments, encouragement, and ideas, can also help. Compliments and a future focus (instead of the past) keep the work positive and solution focused.

130. C: While no single factor can account for all vulnerability, genetics appears to play a significant role. Other potential factors include gender, development stage, social environment, and culture or ethnicity. Known environmental risk factors include: unemployment or underemployment, high neighborhood crime rates, prevalence of illicit drugs (including cost and ease of procurement), poor housing (dilapidated or overcrowded), peer pressures, community attitudes, and low social achievement expectations. Known cultural or ethnic/racial risk factors include: minority status, discrimination based on race, intergenerational assimilation disparity, language and cultural barriers to social services and health care, poor educational achievement, cultural devaluation in the dominant society, and cultural alienation. Known family risk factors include: poor bonding, highly chaotic home, family conflict and violence, financial strain, home stress, parental substance abuse, parental neglect, and parental mental illness. Known emotional or behavioral risk factors include: low self-esteem, aggression, rebelliousness, high independence needs, nonconformity, shyness, delinquency, emotional problems, suicidality, relationship problems, using gateway drugs, and academic and drop-out problems.

131. D: Where a high-risk home life exists, a minor child will fare better if he or she is able to distance him- or herself from the troubled home, and if he or she can develop a talent, skill, or something that is valued by others in the social circle and community. Other factors that are protective against substance abuse and addiction are: community factors—a positive neighborhood, low levels of crime, adequate housing, and high rates of employment; family environment—adequate parental attention (especially during the first year of life), a nurturing family with appropriate structure, parents who encourage learning, and adequate household income; innate strengths—physically healthy, positive temperament and emotional well-being, and above-average intelligence; personality—flexible and adaptable, upbeat nature, self-disciplined, easygoing temperament, reasonable expectations, and good problem-solving skills.

132. A: The strengths that combine to produce resiliency include: (1) insight (asking essential questions, accepting honest answers, and thereby developing a mature understanding of self, others, and situations); (2) independence (balancing proper personal boundaries against the need for family bonds and affection and separating from the family if needed); (3) wholesome relationships (finding substitute parents or mentors, as needed, with balanced attachments); (4) initiative (able to accomplish goals and tasks from which is drawn proper self-esteem and a pleasure in achievement that promotes ongoing growth and development); (5) creativity or humor (imaginative creativity to make nothing into something positive); (6) humor (the ability to laugh at oneself and circumstances so as to turn something negative into nothing); and (7) morality (a well-informed conscience that serves and alleviates suffering in others). Fostering these strengths in children, youth, and adults can help them develop into highly resilient individuals.

133. B: Consequently, this group tends to delay treatment, which leads to less care overall. Deference to parents and the need to sustain family pride are at times problematic variables.

Religious ceremonies and traditional celebrations are central cultural components, and alcohol use is typically expected at such events. On average, 40 percent of this group report alcohol use, and 5 percent report illicit substance use, with the highest rates among Puerto Ricans and the lowest among Cubans. Spanish-language groups and counselors are important contributions to the treatment process. Locating Spanish-speaking twelve-step groups can also make a substantial difference to positive, long-term outcomes.

134. C: However, the overall group is remarkably diverse, coming not only from Africa, but also from Bermuda, South America, the Caribbean, and Canada. While most U.S.-born African Americans have shared experiences in terms of institutionalized racism and a relatively recent history with segregation and a distant recognition of slavery, many foreign-born Africans who reside in America have remarkably different experiences. Many grew up in countries with a majority black population and governments made up mostly of blacks. On average, 34 percent of African Americans report using alcohol (compared with 40 percent of Hispanics and 51 percent of whites. Further, only 9 percent of African American youth reported alcohol use, compared with 16 percent or more among white and Hispanic populations. African American use of illicit substances is similar to that of whites (6 percent) but higher than among Hispanics (5 percent). Unmet treatment needs are at 25 percent (Hispanics are at 23 percent), which is twice that as among whites.

135. D: Alcohol-related deaths are over three times the national average. Among those between the ages of twelve and seventeen, illicit substance abuse was 22 percent—a rate higher and at younger ages than any other group. Although only 20 percent of Native American live on reservations or trust lands, issues of poverty and unemployment as well as a culture relatively tolerant of alcohol and substance use have contributed to these troubling figures. There are 562 separate tribal entities recognized by the Bureau of Indian Affairs, and thus generalizations should be avoided. A tendency to use native healing traditions to treat substance abuse has also created further complexity. Some tribes are making efforts to push for alcohol-free activities, and recognition of the need to address the problem is growing. Considerable further progress needs to be made, and culturally sensitive programs should figure prominently in these efforts.

136. B: Currently, this group comprises some 4 percent of the total U.S. population and 25 percent of the total foreign-born population (nine of ten were born on foreign soil). The majority of this heterogeneous group (more than half) live in only three states (California, Hawaii, and New York). Approximately 28 percent of Asian and Pacific Islanders report alcohol use, though only 3 percent report the use of illicit substances. This is the lowest rate of illicit substance abuse among all groups. Further, only 7 percent of adolescents in this group report alcohol use, as compared with 16 percent or more among whites, Hispanic or Latino, and Native American youth. However, it should be noted that there is great variation among various Asian and Pacific Islander groups. For example, illicit substance abuse rates by selected intragroup members are: Chinese (1 percent), Asian Indians (2 percent), Japanese (5 percent), and Koreans (7 percent). Consequently, careful assessments will be required.

137. B: A discharge summary encompasses: (1) client demographics and general profile; (2) symptoms at admission; (3) interventions provided and outcomes realized; (4) critical incidents that occurred and resolution processes for each; (5) treatment goal progress and obstacles to progress; and (6) recommendations for further treatment in light of all treatment program events and progress. A continuing care plan encompasses: (1) options based on client's successes and residual needs; (2) appropriate resource linkages (food, housing, education, family needs, and legal issues); and (3) schedules for group meetings, twelve-step programs, and counseling, as well as other interventions. The discharge summary depicts what was done, why, and outcomes, as well as future recommendations. A continuing care plan explores options, identifies resources of benefit, and serves to schedule and coordinate all aftercare meetings and services.

138. A: During the annual evaluation, two key elements of evaluation are process and outcome. Process follows: drug testing results, individual or group interventions offered (session attendance, topics covered, etc.), and treatment plan formulation rationale and modifications. Each area covered is eventually aggregated into a total agency intervention and success or efficacy scores. Outcome addresses primary program goals and the level of success realized for each. Key indices include: attainment and maintenance of sobriety, educational or vocational goals, progress in behavioral goals, and degrees of success in family and social goals. Documentation (or charting) involves recording treatment interventions, together with levels of success, challenges, and the type and rationale for any modifications in interventions, goals, and success measures. Current law prevents recording human immunodeficiency virus (HIV) status in a regular chart, and counselors should avoid recording information that might be used to penalize or harm a client, should law enforcement discover or obtain the record.

139. C: The most effective and influential treatment plans are those designed by both the client and a counselor working in concert with each other. This approach provides optimal buy-in for the client and the greatest clarity for counseling staff. The treatment plan should include an action plan for recovery that covers the duration of time prior to the next treatment plan review. Once complete, both the client and counselor should signify their joint commitment by mutually affixing their dated signatures to the current plan. Following this, the document should be reviewed and signed by the supervisor and medical director. Updates to the treatment plan should be provided at any time that major changes occur in the client's progress, behavior, or motivations.

140. C: The types of program service modalities most commonly include: (1) residential; (2) outpatient; (3) day care habilitative; (4) narcotic treatment program; and (5) perinatal. Common goal areas include: (1) substance use; (2) medical issues; (3) legal issues; (4) psychosocial progress; (5) educational or vocational; (6) employment; (7) financial; (8) discharge; and (9) other. Progress notes addressing the goals should include references to the specific area being targeted by the goals or action plans. In the progress note, the counselor writes out what they did to facilitate accomplishment of the goal. The counselor should also record objective impressions regarding the client's behavior, attitudes, and efforts to achieve long- and short-term objectives found in the treatment plan.

141. C: The concept of nonmaleficence is an ethical principle drawn from the biomedical literature. It refers to the ancient medical tenant *Primum Non Nocere* (Latin: first, do no harm—i.e., never make a problem worse). Medication-assisted treatment of opioid addiction has been challenged as enlarging or at least perpetuating an addictive problem. However, given the serious risks of illicit opioid use, ethicists have dismissed these concerns.

Other key ethical principles are: (2) beneficence—working for the benefit and well-being of all clients (e.g., proper diagnosis, evidence-based treatments, etc.); (3) autonomy—often referred to as self-determination, this principle emphasizes respect for client rights to make well-informed choices that meet their own desires and life goals (it assumes a client has been fully informed of all risks and benefits of available options, and properly understands them); (4) justice—requires treatment providers to act fairly, equally, and equitably, especially when resources are limited; and (5) fidelity—faithfulness in honoring commitments and obligations (not abandoning clients, making and supporting proper referrals, etc.).

142. B: While empathy is important, it is necessary to find balance in working with clients who have suffered considerable past trauma and abuse. Becoming overly drawn in can cause the counselor to lose objectivity, become inappropriately emotional (angry, vengeful, etc.), and miss the opportunities to help the client move through and past his or her painful history. This can be particularly problematic if the counselor shares a similar past, which may easily lend to over-involvement in the presenting issues. In like manner, it also important that the counselor not be too dispassionate and detached, failing to allow the client to emotionally vent and unburden him- or herself. Typically, however, it is not necessary for a client to be prodded into revealing his or her past in minute detail. Rather, proper disclosure to the level needed for understanding is all that is necessary. It is important for counselors not to assume abuse from every symptom. As abuse in common in substance abusers, it is easy to infer abuse where it didn't exist—especially with clients who are overly eager to please their counselor.

143. C: Clients with a past history of abuse often have painful and difficult memories and feelings about relationships. In particular, abuse often occurred in close relationships where the client should have been safe and protected. As the therapeutic bond in counseling grows, emerging feelings of closeness and trust can often trigger the complex feelings of the past. In so doing, these painful past feelings may be projected onto the counselor, causing the relationship to deteriorate. Clients may cope by trying to avoid dealing with the past, or they may maneuver the counselor into interactive patterns that replicate the past (e.g., caretaker, abuser, neglector, etc.). Care should be used not be manipulated, however unintentionally, into a client's past relational roles. This is best accomplished by maintaining objectivity, avoiding being drawn into offered roles, and by dealing directly and openly with any transference issues that arise.

144. B: These feelings can arise out of the counselor's past, or they can emerge in reaction to transference issues brought into the counselor–client relationship by the client. Unhealthy countertransference occurs when unresolved problems and feelings are projected onto the client. Absent clear boundaries and careful self-awareness, the counselor can lose the objectivity necessary to meet the client's needs and understand emerging issues. Countertransference is not the same as reacting to clear presentations from the client (e.g., positively when the client is pleasant and responsive and negatively if the client has a difficult personality). Diligent self-awareness can help the counselor identify the source of feelings along with the nature of the feelings and can help the counselor better serve the client, who may be evoking similar feelings and many others. When client needs and countertransference run together, the counselor may open up past issues prematurely and thereby compromise the client's welfare.

145. D: Counselors working with substance abusers are often exposed to traumatic narratives from clients with extensive histories of abuse (especially parent to child) and life chaos. When unrelieved, these narratives can accumulate and lead to posttraumatic stress disorder (PTSD)-like symptoms in counselors—difficulty concentrating, diminished affect, irritability, troubling dreams, compromised sleep, intrusive thoughts, free-floating anxiety, and so on. Accompanying feelings of anger, fear, or helplessness are common.

The result can be counselor numbness and detachment, unconsciously dismissing client feelings and traumas, or overinvestment with parent-like caregiving or even inappropriate efforts at problem solving, rescuing, and failing to guide the client to essential growth. In these situations, counselors must seek supportive supervision and guidance to overcome emotional burdens and problematic responses.

146. A: Working with substance abuse clients can expose counselors to high emotions, great volatility, emotionally traumatic narratives of abuse, and so on. Over time, counselors can develop symptoms of compassion fatigue, apathy, and discouragement. Left unchecked, such feelings can compromise the counselor's skills, erode relationships, and can lead to a greatly shortened professional career and diminished personal life success. To combat burnout, counselors should: (1) avoid working in isolation; (2) maintain close supervisory support; (3) look for debriefing opportunities; (4) carry a varied caseload to minimize overload in one emotional area; (5) avoid overload in the number of cases being seen; (6) keep personal and professional life separated; (7) take appropriate vacations and time off; and (8) consider attending a counselor support group. Psychotherapy can also help the counselor professionally and personally in such situations.

147. B: Clients with dense abuse histories often have difficulty establishing boundaries and have intense needs for approval, affection, and nurturing. Counselors can easily fall into trying to meet these needs, even while finding the relationship expanding to the point of role overload. To avoid this, counselors need to establish a treatment frame that helps set up and maintain reasonable boundaries. Key features of the treatment frame include: (1) an awareness that overinvestment fosters client dependency; (2) an understanding that clients must take responsibility for their own lives to grow; (3) establishing appointment times and durations in advance to limit encroachment; (4) enforcing start and closing session times; (5) refraining from giving out one's home phone number; (6) canceling sessions if the client is intoxicated; (7) limiting all contacts to the therapy session; (8) preventing intimate (sexual) boundary misinterpretations; (9) terminating if threats or acts of violence are experienced; and (10) insisting on proper and timely payment of session fees.

148. C: Failing to set proper and consistent boundaries may initially appeal to a client, but uncertain boundaries will inevitably lead to client uncertainty, anxiety, and misunderstandings, which ultimately erode trust. Clients with troubled parent–child relationships often find themselves in other abusive relationships. As the experiences with these problematic relationships grow increasingly negative, such clients often become overly suspicious and distrusting of even therapeutic relationships. As the counselor remains consistent, committed, and balanced, especially in times of crisis, client trust will grow, and the client can begin experiencing and building the essential features needed for trusting relationships. Contributing greatly is the unconditional positive regard and nonjudgmental attitude the client experiences from the counselor.

149. B: Clients with a history of substance abuse often have unmet developmental issues, along with issues of confused emotions due to substance influences and distortions due to histories of intimate abuse. Many are unfamiliar with virtually any trusting and caring relationship, having largely been subjected to relationships of shame, guilt, fear, and anger. As trust in the counselor grows, these feelings can easily be misinterpreted as feelings of romantic love for the counselor. This can be compounded when abstinence leads to a distorted substitution of fantasies and romantic thoughts for substance intoxication. In response, counselors must maintain impeccable boundaries, and consider: (1) addressing the feelings openly; (2) turning the client's feelings toward other nonsexual relationships; and (3) teaching the client to differentiate between feeling good and feeling sexual desire. To maintain safety and balance, it is important for counselors to disclose such situations to a trusted colleague in order to properly balance the situation and maintain safety.

150. D: Every licensing body has ethical prohibitions against a counselor becoming sexually involved with a client. The likelihood of such an ethical breach being reported is very high, and the results inevitably lead to loss of employment and licensure. Further, many states have criminal statutes that would apply, and both civil and criminal prosecution are very likely. Most importantly, however, the damage done to the client can be profound when yet another meaningful relationship fails to be safe. A client's seductive behavior is no protection from this, as many see sexual favors as the only way they can earn or feel to deserve a positive relationship. Counselors must profoundly

guard against such conduct. Many feel male counselors should not treat female sexual abuse victims, and a client preference in counselor gender should be honored. Where circumstances allow or require otherwise, however, a male counselor who maintains safety can provide a client with new positive male role model and thus help the client further along in recovery.

Thank You

We at Mometrix would like to extend our heartfelt thanks to you, our friend and patron, for allowing us to play a part in your journey. It is a privilege to serve people from all walks of life who are unified in their commitment to building the best future they can for themselves.

The preparation you devote to these important testing milestones may be the most valuable educational opportunity you have for making a real difference in your life. We encourage you to put your heart into it—that feeling of succeeding, overcoming, and yes, conquering will be well worth the hours you've invested.

We want to hear your story, your struggles and your successes, and if you see any opportunities for us to improve our materials so we can help others even more effectively in the future, please share that with us as well. **The team at Mometrix would be absolutely thrilled to hear from you!** So please, send us an email (support@mometrix.com) and let's stay in touch.

If you feel as though you need additional help, please check out the other resources we offer:

Study Guide: http://MometrixStudyGuides.com/ADC

Flashcards: http://MometrixFlashcards.com/ADC